MARCUS SCHNECK

YOUR BACKYARD WILDLIFE YEAR

How to attract birds,
butterflies, and other animals
every month of the year.

Foreword by
Roger Tory Peterson

Rodale Press, Inc.
Emmaus, Pennsylvania

OUR MISSION

We publish books that empower people's lives.

RODALE BOOKS

Quarto Publishing Staff
  Senior Editor: Sally MacEachearn
  Editor: Barbara Haynes
  Editorial Director: Mark Dartford
  Senior Art Editor: Anne Fisher
  Designer: Neville Graham
  Picture Researcher: Giulia Hetherington
  Cover Designer: Neville Graham
  Interior Illustrators: Ann Savage, Elisabeth Dowle
  Art Director: Moira Clinch

Rodale Press Staff
  Editorial Director, Home and Garden:
    Margaret Lydic Balitas
  Managing Editor: Ellen Phillips
  Copy Editor: Nancy Nickum Bailey
  Editor-in-Chief: William Gottlieb

If you have any questions or comments concerning this book, please write to:
Rodale Press, Inc.
Book Readers' Service
33 East Minor Street
Emmaus, PA 18098

Library of Congress Cataloging-in-Publication Data
  Schneck, Marcus.
    Your backyard wildlife year: how to attract birds, butterflies,
    and other animals every month of the year / Marcus Schneck.
        P.   cm.
    Includes bibliographical references (p.   ) and index.
    ISBN 0–87596–706–X (hardcover: alk. paper).
    1. Gardening to attract wildlife. 2. Wildlife attracting.
  I. Title.
  OL59.S37 1996
  635.9'6 — dc20   95–25983

Distributed in the book trade by St. Martin's Press

2 4 6 8 10 9 7 5 3 1

Typeset by Type Technique, London, England
Manufactured in Singapore by Bright Arts (Singapore) Pte Ltd.
Printed by Leefung-Asco Printers, China

To my son, Casey, and a future
filled with wild things

CONTENTS

FOREWORD

How I would have benefited from this book when I acquired my first property in suburbia near Washington, D.C.! And even more when I moved into the more expansive surroundings of my home and studio in the Connecticut hills, where I have now lived for 40 years. Many of the things that Marcus Schneck outlines I have done – or stumbled upon through trial and error – but this book would have saved me a lot of time. In its pages there are ever so many tidbits that my wife, Ginny, and I must try.

The important thing to remember is that we live in a complex world where there are no simple answers. Many of us are trying to live our lives as a part of nature, not apart from nature. Most of us want deer, but what if they eat our favorite garden flowers? And what if we use sprays? I do not because I love butterflies. We cannot have butterflies if we spray their caterpillars, those little grub-like critters that almost no one likes because they eat holes in leaves. If we spare them, they pupate into a chrysalis that is like a coffin. Seemingly dead – in a crypt – each one eventually emerges as a beautiful butterfly that dances about like an angel, but for a much-too-brief period. What a transformation!

Their nocturnal counterparts – the big moths, the saturnids, sphinxes and underwings – are virtually gone where we live in Connecticut because of the spraying for gypsy moths that went on 15 or 20 years ago. Because of these biocides and the resultant lack of enough moths, we have almost lost our summer resident whip-poor-wills and nighthawks.

It can even be argued that bird feeding can have its negative side effects. Cardinals, titmice, red-bellied woodpeckers and several other "southern" birds have extended their ranges northward because their winter survival has been enhanced by our handout, and others like chickadees, nuthatches and many woodpeckers have also benefited. But the butterflies and other insects on our property have declined, I think, because of greater consumption of their larvae by these feeder addicts. So when the orioles, tanagers, vireos and warblers return from the tropics, they find leaner pickings of insects on our property. Where there is a plus, there is often a minus.

But by planning your strategy month by month, you may be able to balance things out, providing more food, water and protective shelter for everything, big and small, while giving yourself a window into the environment. Although we live in a world of rule makers, it sometimes pays to take a chance on an offbeat idea. If it works, fine; if not, forget it. I know that Ginny and I will gain a lot from Mr Schneck's organized month-by-month plan.

Roger Tory Peterson

INTRODUCTION

Many books have been written on the subject of backyard wildlife gardening including my own previous work, *Your Backyard Wildlife Garden*. But I have never encountered a book that is packed with loads of projects for the backyard wildlife garden. That is exactly what I have tried to bring to life in this new work. Here I have pulled together the best projects developed through my Backyard Wildlife Network and other projects I have developed for my own backyard habitat well before the Network was even a thought. Years of experience with wildlife in the backyard habitat are condensed into these fun, fast, easy-to-make projects.

This book comes at a particularly critical time in our history. The large public parks, preserves, and gamelands set aside for wildlife are going to be very few and far between from this point forward. We will see very few Yellowstone-like parks created in our future. And, as I write this, growing numbers of our fellow Americans have come to the conclusion that we can no longer afford to set aside even a small portion of our lands for wildlife and recreation. Large-scale surveys show the incredible value the majority of us still place on wildlife and wild places and the economic value of these critters and these special sites. But in spite of the survey results, these factions see only the immediate dollars that can be stripped and wrenched from the land.

These trends give our backyard wildlife habitats an increased importance in preserving the critters that remain. Our homemade habitats probably will never rescue an endangered species from the brink, but the sum total of the properties that we are willing to commit to wildlife use most definitely can help to keep many, many species away from that precipitous edge.

None of us needs to give our entire property back to wildlife. Human uses, ranging from play areas to lawns, must be considered when decisions about property uses are made. Nearly all of the projects discussed in the following chapters are small-scale, needing only a few feet or yards of land. The critters will respond, eager to take advantage of whatever niches we offer here and there.

HOW TO USE THIS BOOK

This book is organized in a month-by-month format, so it's really easy to use — just turn to the current month and you'll find a range of projects and wildlife-related activities. I have made sure that the projects fall in the most appropriate month for you to complete them and put them to work in your own backyard wildlife habitat.

However, with a few obvious exceptions, any of the projects can be done at any time during the year. You probably don't want to be digging soil and working with water, as needed to install a minipond, in the dead of winter. But there is no reason that you

can't pull the winter roosting box for birds project out of November and make it during July; that way it will be ready in time to welcome its winter residents.

Each chapter begins with a monthly activity checklist. This is your guide to yard, garden, and wildlife-related activities that are appropriate to that month. I have tried to make this as accurate as possible by matching activities to the USDA plant hardiness zones. And, while these special "to do" lists do include many traditional yard and garden chores, they also emphasize activities that will benefit the critters.

1 Monthly activity checklist – your guide to yard, garden and wildlife-related activities

2 Activities for each month vary depending on your USDA plant hardiness zone

3 Projects are placed in the most appropriate month for you to make them

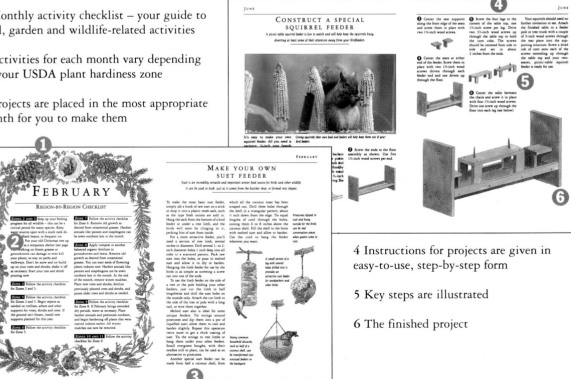

4 Instructions for projects are given in easy-to-use, step-by-step form

5 Key steps are illustrated

6 The finished project

USDA PLANT HARDINESS ZONE MAP

Zone maps, such as the USDA Plant Hardiness Zone Map below that has been followed throughout this book, are for determining which perennials, trees, shrubs, grasses and so on will survive the winter in your area. Zone maps are great for giving you a general picture — if you live in Zone 2, you don't want to spend time and money on a plant that's hardy only to Zone 7. However, in using such maps, it is critical to remember that within every zone on the map there are microclimates created by localized conditions that may make your neighborhood cooler or warmer than the zone suggested by the map. Even within the microclimates, there will be conditions that create yard-size, or even smaller, areas of quite different conditions. So don't "go by the book" — combine the map's recommendations with your own knowledge of conditions in your backyard.

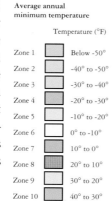

Average annual minimum temperature

Temperature (°F)

Zone 1	Below -50°
Zone 2	-40° to -50°
Zone 3	-30° to -40°
Zone 4	-20° to -30°
Zone 5	-10° to -20°
Zone 6	0° to -10°
Zone 7	10° to 0°
Zone 8	20° to 10°
Zone 9	30° to 20°
Zone 10	40° to 30°

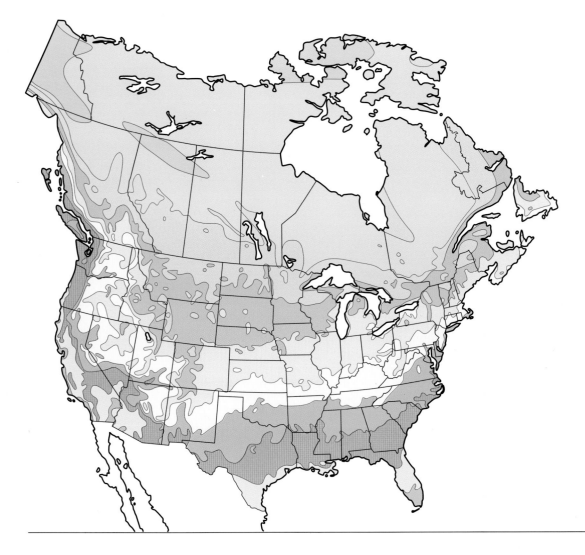

JANUARY

REGION-BY-REGION CHECKLIST

ZONES 2 AND 3 Activity at the bird and wildlife feeders continues to build as winter goes on. Take advantage of every new snowfall – it's an opportunity to learn more about the travels and habits of the wildlife using your backyard habitat, since it's easy to read their tracks in the new-fallen snow. Keep water sources open. Walking on frozen grasses or groundcovers can damage or even kill your plants, so stay on paths and walkways. Check your winter mulches regularly; repair and replace as necessary. Keep the mulch pulled back from tree trunks so rodents can't girdle them. Don't let snow and ice become too heavy for your trees and shrubs.

ZONE 4 Follow the activity checklist for Zones 2 and 3. Find time to prune woody vines.

ZONE 5 Follow the activity checklist for Zone 4. Inspect bulbs in storage for rot, or drying out. Compost bad bulbs.

ZONE 6 Follow the activity checklist for Zone 5. Sow seeds indoors for early-blooming perennials and annuals, and for later-blooming perennials and annuals if they're slow-growing.

ZONE 7 Follow the activity checklist for Zone 6. Prune summer-flowering trees and shrubs. Plant trees and shrubs.

ZONE 8 Depending on last fall's migration, uncommon (for this zone) bird species may be spending the winter in your backyard habitat. Use your field guide to see how many you can identify. Cut back grasses as necessary. Fertilize grasses and emerging perennials and annuals. Sow seeds of summer-blooming perennials indoors. Plant trees and shrubs. Prune hedges.

ZONE 9 Follow the activity checklist for Zone 8. Plant new grasses and groundcovers. Plant hardy annuals and perennials outdoors. Deadhead winter-blooming annuals. Prune summer-flowering trees and shrubs.

ZONES 10 AND 11 Follow the activity checklist for Zone 9. Plant all annuals and perennials outdoors.

PLAN THE YEAR AHEAD

January is the perfect month to sit back with some hot chocolate or coffee

and a plateful of your favorite cookies, in the comfortable warmth of your home,

and take a look at your plans for the coming year.

Start by deciding what you'd like to do in your backyard habitat, then draw up an activity checklist. Don't forget to pace yourself, and give your plans a realistic review to make sure you're not being too ambitious. After all, you want time to enjoy the fruits of your effort.

First, map what you have

On a piece of paper, draw a rough map of your property. You don't need to be a professional mapmaker or artist — after all, nobody's going to be grading your work. First, try to outline the general shape of your property. Indicate its dimensions — an estimate is good enough. Note the location and size of your house and other buildings with rectangles, or whatever shapes are appropriate. Indicate your trees and shrubs with circles, noting the species and approximate sizes (height and trunk diameter). If your property is large or you have a lot of trees, it might be easier to list the trees and shrubs and their sizes on a separate piece of paper, and then key the numbers to your tree and shrub list. Indicate any dead trees that are still standing (snags) with trunk diameters of 6 inches or more and note the trunk diameter for each. Indicate any dead trees that have fallen and been left in place. Both snags and fallen logs make excellent habitats for a wide variety of wildlife.

Map your flower beds and vines just as you did with your trees and shrubs. Draw in your walkways and paths as close to scale as you can. Sketch in ponds, streams, birdbaths and other sources of water. Note the location, height off the ground, and types of wildlife feeders, birdfeeders, bat houses and nestboxes. Indicate the type of seed or food you use in each of your feeders. Again, you might want to use numbers and list the content and brand on a separate piece of paper with the numbers keyed in. Indicate areas of open lawn. Then add any special features, such as a deck, steep slope, perpetually wet area, picnic table or swimming pool.

On a separate piece of paper, draw the outline of your property at the center and indicate the current land uses of surrounding properties. For example, neighboring properties might include a cornfield, home with open lawn, woodlot, stream or wooded park.

The best way to start mapping your property is to fill in all the large elements — such as the house or trees — in your yard and the surrounding areas.

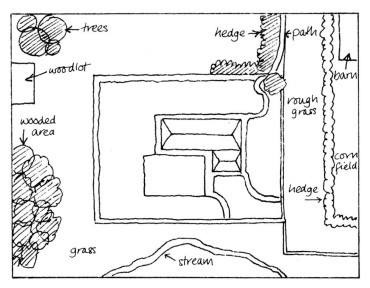

11

List key habitat features

Now you have serviceable, and rather detailed, maps of your property and its surroundings as they currently exist. Your next step is to fill in the following lists and answer any questions on a separate piece of paper. Don't worry if you can't come up with the requested number of responses for any of the lists. Just try to be as thorough and complete as you can.

• List the ten bird species you are already attracting in the greatest numbers. List the additional bird species you would like to attract. (Your list should include only species that are native to your region and to the type of habitat in which your property is located.) List the bird species you would like to attract less of, like starlings and grackles. Repeat this process three more times – once for mammals, once for reptiles and amphibians and once for insects and spiders.

• List any species (bird, mammal, reptile, amphibian, insect or spider) that your neighbors or people just down the street are attracting and that you are not but would like to. List possible reasons why your neighbors are attracting those species. Ask your neighbors for their ideas on why they are attracting those species.

• List in detail any problems you are experiencing in your backyard habitat for which you would like to have solutions.

• Create a wish list of features you would like to include in your backyard habitat. Focus on things you really want, like a water garden or rugosa rose hedge.

• Estimate the distance (in feet or yards, if feasible) from your property to the nearest stream, creek, river, canal, swamp, pond or lake. Is there a natural

connection between that body of water or wetland and your property? A natural connection would be something like a patch of woods, fencerow or weedy drainage ditch. If no such connection exists, can you think of any way you could create a connection?

• Do you have any artificial sources of water on your property like a pool, pond or birdbath? List them. Do any of these incorporate moving or dripping water? Are any of your water sources easily accessible to critters that can't fly or climb?

Spread your answer sheets for the first four checklists out on a table, a desk or the floor. Carefully look over the lists you have created and begin to combine all the features you want to add and wildlife you want to attract onto one, new list. Don't worry about putting them into any special order. After you have written out the new list, go back over the items and rank them from the most important/most needed/most wanted to the least, assigning the appropriate number to each.

Start with your number one priority item and begin thinking about how you might accomplish that. Good natural

You can design a backyard wildlife habitat to attract many different birds, butterflies and other critters. Decide what kinds of wildlife you want in your garden before you start to plan.

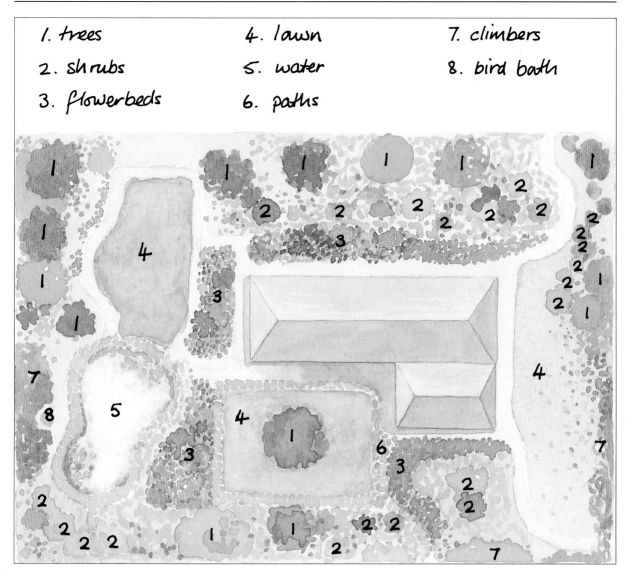

1. trees
2. shrubs
3. flowerbeds
4. lawn
5. water
6. paths
7. climbers
8. bird bath

history, landscaping reference and how-to books come in very handy at this point. (A good place to start is the book you're holding now.)

If you're trying to attract a new species, a field guide or similar book that discusses habits and habitats in detail will hold many crucial clues. (Turn to "Recommended Reading" on page 157 for some of the best.) Here's a tip: Take a close look at your answers to the questions about water. Now see what the books have to say about the species' need for water or wetland environments. I've found that one of the biggest roadblocks to attracting creatures otherwise common to an area is the lack of water or water in the form the species needs.

When you start working up a plan of action for one or more of the top items on your priority list, take a look at the maps you've drawn of your property and its surroundings to see if you can really carry out your plan. Finally, where's the best place to put the feature?

Your initial plan for your backyard habitat can be as simple or as complex as you want. Remember, you're not trying to be a professional landscape architect. You just need something you can work from.

CREATE NEW LIFE FOR AN OLD CHRISTMAS TREE

Designed to get your New Year's resolutions off to a good start, this project combines recycling and providing winter shelter.

It's the first weekend of the new year, and the family Christmas tree is beginning to show signs of wear. Needles are turning up throughout the house. The dog has slurped more than his share of water from the tree holder. It's painfully clear that the dreaded finishing touch to the holiday season is upon us: It's time to take down the Christmas tree.

But that old evergreen has a new life ahead and can provide an easy lesson in recycling for your kids or grand-children. The Christmas tree can now become a winter shelter for wildlife in your backyard. Take it down just as you always do, but instead of dragging it to the curb for the trash pick-up, take it into the backyard. Lay it on its side in a location where it will provide cover for wildlife and viewing opportunities for your family. Secure the tree in position by driving four stakes into the ground around it – one on each side at the top and one on each side at the bottom – and tie the tree to the stakes with strong cord. This will prevent the strong winter winds from rolling the tree into the neighbor's driveway.

In the cold temperatures of the next few months, the tree will hold most of its needles. By spring, when only its branching skeleton remains, run the tree through a mulcher for free recycled wood chips.

You can monitor the wildlife that visits this temporary shelter by checking for tracks in fresh snowfalls during the season.

Just because the holidays are gone doesn't mean that there's no life left in your old Christmas tree. In your backyard, it can provide shelter for many small critters throughout the remaining cold winter months. Recycling the tree like this is one of the nicest reasons for choosing a real Christmas tree.

TALK IT OVER FIRST

One of the most important things you can do during the "slow" time of the year outdoors is to win your neighbors over to your way of thinking on the subject of wildlife in your backyard and, naturally, in their backyards, too.

COTTONTAIL
RABBIT

Getting the neighbors involved in your wildlife projects is the best way to avoid problems *and* attract more wildlife. For, as surprising as it may be, there are a great many people who prefer to have their huge expanses of costly, chemical-dependent lawn uncluttered with what they see as the riffraff of the animal kingdom. They see nothing but damage, more work and more expense in the same creatures you love. Recent years have seen an amazing array of ordinances, regulations and tactics brought to bear against the owners of backyard wildlife habitats. Everything from noxious weed laws to lawn height restrictions and nuisance animal laws have been employed against us.

Many of the situations I've seen over the years could have been prevented, or at least lessened to a great degree, if the neighbors had been consulted in advance. An explanation of the lofty goal of giving just a little something back to the birds and other creatures who were evicted to make way for human housing can be enlightening for some homeowners. A discussion of the basic concepts involved in gardening for wildlife (note the phrasing here) is another effective possibility. Tell them about some of the more desirable and less destructive creatures you plan to attract, like hummingbirds and butterflies. Agree in advance to do whatever it takes to solve any problems that arise because of the presence of wildlife in the area. Take this book with you and share the beautiful photographs of delightful creatures in backyard settings and the exciting projects you – and they – can create to attract them.

The eastern cottontail is one of the most adaptable backyard critters – it can be found across much of the country. It will

While many neighbors will appreciate your efforts to attract appealing species like this American goldfinch, there are still those who see birds in the backyard as a messy bother.

live in any backyard where adequate shelter and cover are provided near grass, clover and weeds, the mainstays of its diet.

WHAT IS A NICHE?

If attracting wildlife is your goal, start with the animal's needs

from its own perspective. Here's how to see plants from a bird's

(or chipmunk's) eye view.

Every living creature occupies a certain niche within its environment. Within that niche, it satisfies its basic needs in four specific categories: food, water, shelter from enemies and the elements and protected places to give birth and raise young. Some types of wildlife may fulfill their needs in more than one category from a single plant species. But in one way or another, all four categories must be fulfilled for the survival of the animal in a given place.

To find the preferred habitat and four niche categories for whatever type of wildlife you want to attract, check out a good field guide. (See "Recommended Reading" on page 157 for some suggestions.) That basic information applied to plant selection most often will give you what you need to know to attract the desired wildlife species.

Create a 3-D landscape

There's one more element you'll need to factor in when you're trying to attract wildlife – the varied heights and depths of the plants in your landscape. This is because a species niche must also be seen as three dimensional where wildlife can take advantage of adequate space, both on the ground and above it.

Aboveground space can range from grass height to above the treetops. For example, most birds have rather specific height requirements for nesting.

There must also be room to spread out. Every wildlife species needs a given home range large enough to satisfy the

four basic needs and provide the amount of space individual members generally prefer to leave between themselves and others of their species. In addition, many species have a decided preference for a certain layout or mix of elements they require to satisfy their needs, such as trees, shrubs and weeds or tall grass.

Luckily for us, though, most wildlife species will respond to any attempt to fulfill their basic needs. Only when plant selection and a water source are not attracting the wildlife we hoped it would, is there a need to consider the deeper factors.

The red fox is an omnivore, so it can find food and water in a wide range of environments. Weedy, brush-covered trails and large open areas provide cover for the fox, while it uses existing burrows or concealed spots for shelter.

LIVE IN HARMONY WITH WILDLIFE

When you invite wildlife into your backyard, remember that they remain wild things.

Some of their habits are just plain infuriating.

Many schemes have been devised over the years to protect our yards from unwanted wildlife attacks. Some don't work. Most present us with mixed results. Here are a few effective tactics.

For any small-scale problem, from a single shrub to your entire vegetable garden, enclosure is the solution. Large vegetable gardens and even farmers' fields have been protected right in the heart of the heaviest whitetail deer populations with proper fencing. The key to effective enclosure is fencing with a mesh spacing of no more than 2 inches. For strong tunnelers, like the groundhog, you'll need to protect both above- and underground to a height and depth of at least 3 feet. For high-jumpers, like the deer, the critical dimension is height, and the minimum necessary to keep them out is 9 feet. For climbers like squirrels, the regular fencing may need to be topped with a strand of electric fence.

For aerial assaults, only full enclosure of the plant or area to be protected will be truly effective. Frame supports with walls and a roof of fence are very effective in protecting grape vines, blueberries, bush cherries, and other small fruits. When you need to protect an individual plant, mesh bird netting is a great deterrent to critters as large as deer, as well as birds. Bird netting works well on cherry trees and strawberry beds.

For the most comprehensive look at an incredible collection of deterrent,

repellent and diversionary tactics for many different species of wildlife, I recommend the book *Please Don't Eat My Garden!* by Nancy McCord. (See "Recommended Reading" on page 157.) It is the most thorough examination of this specialized subject on the market today.

Physical barriers are a simple, cheap and effective way to protect susceptible plants or gardens from wildlife damage.

BUILD A WINDOWBOX FEEDER

This windowbox feeder provides maximum visibility so you can watch the bird action from a front row seat.

Here's a feeder that brings the birds to you. The length of the feeder (the dimension that runs parallel to the window) can be varied to fit any window. Also, you can add ornamental curves and arches to this basic plan, if you wish.

What you'll need

One ¾-inch-thick, rot-resistant board, cut into:
 One 11 × 22-inch tray piece
 Two 11 × 12-inch roof supports
 Two 11 × 10-inch tray supports
 One 2 × 22-inch back support
One piece of ⅛-inch acrylic sheeting, cut into:
 One 9 × 22-inch roof piece
 One 11¼ × 20¼-inch back piece
Nine 2-inch wood screws
Wood glue
Silicone glue
Chalk

Here's what to do

1 Select one of the long sides of the tray piece to be the back. Cut a ⅛-inch-deep, ⅛-inch-wide saw kerf the entire length of the tray piece, ½ inch in from the back edge.

2 On each of the roof supports, make an angled cut from point A to point B, reducing one of the 11-inch sides on each roof support to 9 inches.

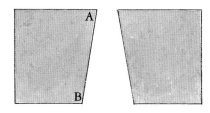

3 On each of the roof supports at the top right-angled corner of the 11-inch side, cut out a ¾-inch × 2-inch rectangle by making cuts from point A to point B and from point C to point B.

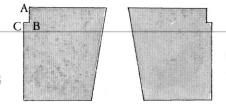

4 Along what will be the inside of each roof support, cut a ⅛-inch-deep, ⅛-inch-wide saw

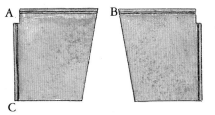

kerf from point A to point B, and from point A to point C.

5 From each of the tray support pieces, cut one 4-inch-wide L, by making cuts from point A to point B and from point C to point B.

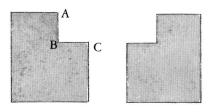

6 Along the entire 22-inch length of the back support, cut one ⅛-inch-deep kerf along the ¾-inch side, and another 1½ inch down on the 2-inch side.

7 Hold the back support with the ¾-inch kerfed side toward you so the 2-inch-wide side with the saw kerf faces down. Along the entire 22-inch length of the bottom of the back support, cut a ⅛-inch-deep, ⅛-inch-wide saw kerf, ½ inch in on the opposite side to that previously kerfed.

8 With the help of a friend or family member, take the tray piece, tray supports and a pencil to the outside of the window where the feeder will eventually be placed. Have your assistant hold the tray piece on top of and level with the window ledge while you move the tray supports around the underside to find the points where they need to be attached to hold the feeder level with the window ledge. Make sure the tray supports also are evenly spaced along the length of the tray, and then mark the appropriate positions with the pencil on the tray piece. Turn the tray piece over and drill two holes through the bottom of the tray piece in the center of the spots you have marked for the tray supports.

9 Attach the roof supports to the tray piece with wood glue and two 2-inch wood screws driven through the underside of the tray piece into the bottom of each roof support. The outside of each roof support must be flush with the ends of the tray piece, and the saw kerfs along the 11-inch side of each roof support must be aligned with the saw kerf along the back of the tray piece.

10 Allow the wood glue to dry for several hours. Then spread silicone glue into the saw kerfs of the roof supports and the tray piece. Slip the acrylic roof piece into the kerfs along the tops of the roof supports. Insert the acrylic back piece into the kerfs along the backs of the roof supports and the tray piece. The fit should be as snug as possible.

11 Spread silicone glue into the saw kerfs of the back support, and wood glue along the edges of the small rectangular openings you cut into the roof supports. Move the back support piece into position in the small rectangular open-ings, making sure that the acrylic roof piece and the acrylic back piece fit snugly into the saw kerfs in the back support. Drive two 2-inch wood screws through the back support into the top of each roof support.

12 Attach the feeder to the window ledge with three 2-inch wood screws down through the tray and into the ledge.

13 On the bottom of the tray, rub chalk around the holes you drilled previously. Move the tray supports into position so they support the weight of the tray against the side of the building. Push them firmly against the chalked holes. Drill ¾-inch-deep holes into the tops of the tray supports, where the chalk has rubbed onto them.

14 Attach the two tray supports to the bottom of the tray with wood glue and two 2-inch wood screws.

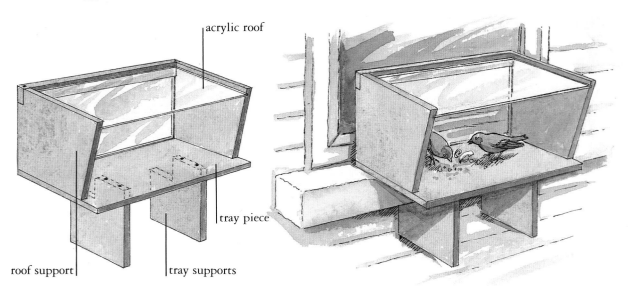

acrylic roof

tray piece

roof support

tray supports

COOK UP RECIPES FOR THE BIRDS

Nearly all recipes for the birds have one of three items as their basic ingredient: beef suet, cornmeal or sand.

A mix of beef suet, cornmeal and sand may not sound too appetizing to us. But for birds, they're gourmet fare. The first two ingredients are the staples, providing high-energy, heat-generating nutrition. The third is more of an add-on to many recipes, providing birds with the grit they need to grind food in their crops.

Suet base and variations

For a very basic, easily adapted recipe, combine beef suet in liquid form with any blend of seeds, according to the species of birds you want to attract. (See "Bringing in the birds" on page 22.)

What you'll need

1 cup liquid beef suet

2 cups seeds (black oil sunflower, black-striped sunflower, cracked corn, niger thistle, shelled peanuts and peanut kernels, safflower, white proso millet) or fruit pieces (apple, blueberry, currant, chopped grape, pear, raisin)

½ tablespoon of sand

Here's what to do

Melt enough beef suet to produce 1 cup in liquid form

(first run it through a meat grinder, or have the butcher do it when you buy it). Let the suet harden and then melt it once again. Blend the seeds or fruit pieces and a half tablespoon of sand thoroughly into the liquid suet. Pour the mixture into molds such as muffin pans or tuna-fish cans that have been emptied and cleaned. Refrigerate until the suet mix forms into hard blocks.

Many birds, such as this female downy woodpecker, relish suet and suet mixtures and will make regular visits to eat them.

Cornmeal base

Another winter treat for the insect eaters uses a cornmeal base.

What you'll need

2 cups whole wheat flour
1 cup cornmeal
½ tablespoon baking soda
1 cup chopped fruit (apples, blueberries, currants, grapes, pears and/or raisins)
½ tablespoon sand
1 cup water
½ cup melted bacon fat

Here's what to do

Mix the dry ingredients thoroughly. Add the water and bacon fat, and blend thoroughly. Spoon the mixture into muffin pans or mini-bread pans. Bake in an oven pre-heated to 350°F for 15 minutes.

For the nonsqueamish, a variation on this basic recipe replaces half the fruit with ½ cup of insects. These could be mealworms, which are available in local pet and bait shops, or the victims of bug zappers collected the summer before in a tray suspended beneath the electronic killer and frozen until needed.

Pizza for the birds

Here's a new recipe that I've just developed for use on feeder trays, or directly on the ground for birds that prefer ground feeding. It's perfect for feeding just about all the bird species in your backyard wildlife habitat.

What you'll need

For the base:
½ teaspoon honey
1 cup warm water
1 packet dry baker's yeast
2 cups all-purpose flour
1 cup cornmeal
2 tablespoons olive oil
¼ cup black oil sunflower seed kernels
¼ cup niger thistle seeds
¼ cup peanut hearts
¼ cup cracked corn
½ tablespoon sand

For the topping:
3 cups melted beef suet
¼ cup black oil sunflower seed kernels
¼ cup niger thistle seeds
½ cup cracked corn
¼ cup peanut hearts
¼ cup whole raisins or currants
¼ cup insects or chopped apples and pears
½ tablespoon sand

Here's what to do

Thoroughly dissolve the honey in the warm water and mix in the yeast. After the yeast has dissolved, let the mixture stand until it begins to bubble. While you're waiting, combine the flour, cornmeal and olive oil. Add the yeast mixture and mix for about five minutes, until a smooth, somewhat sticky dough is formed. Knead the dough by hand on a floured surface, adding pinches of flour as necessary, until you have a smooth breadlike consistency. Place the dough in a bowl, cover it with a towel and let it rise for about an hour. It should double in size during this time. Knead it back to its original size, let it stand another five minutes. Add the seeds, peanut hearts, corn, and sand and knead them throughout the dough for several minutes on a floured surface.

Form the dough into the shape of pizza, with the edges slightly elevated above the center. Place the dough on a pizza pan or cookie sheet that has been sprayed with a non-stick cooking spray like Pam. Stick the pizza dough at several points across its surface with a fork and let it stand for about ten minutes. Bake on the bottom rack in an oven pre-heated to 425°F for about ten minutes, making sure that it doesn't cook beyond the soft-crust stage.

Set the pizza crust aside to cool, and begin making your topping by melting enough suet to make 3 cups. Let this harden and then melt it once again. With the suet again in a liquid state, add the seeds, corn, peanut hearts, fruit pieces and sand, and blend thoroughly. Refrigerate until the suet has hardened to about the consistency of margarine. Spread the suet mixture over the pizza crust, and refrigerate again until the suet has completely hardened.

Serve the "pizza" just as you would any other pizza, flat with the toppings side up.

BRINGING IN THE BIRDS

You'll have the best luck attracting favorite birds to your backyard if you mix the seeds they like best with your suet.

Additional ingredient	Birds attracted
Black oil sunflower seeds	American goldfinch, black-capped chickadee, blue jay, bushtit, cardinal, Carolina chickadee, dark-eyed junco, house finch, mourning dove, pine siskin, purple finch, white-breasted nuthatch
Black-striped sunflower seeds	Cardinal, chipping sparrow, common flicker, common grackle, dark-eyed junco, downy woodpecker, fox sparrow, hairy woodpecker, pine siskin, purple finch, red-breasted nuthatch, scrub jay, song sparrow, tree sparrow, tufted titmouse, white breasted nuthatch, white-crowned sparrow
Niger thistle seeds	American goldfinch, house finch, pine siskin
Cracked corn	Blue jay, Brewer's blackbird, brown-headed cowbird, chipping sparrow, common crow, common grackle, European starling, house sparrow, mourning dove, red-winged blackbird, rufous-sided towhee, scrub jay, song sparrow, tree sparrow, white-crowned sparrow, white-throated sparrow, wood thrush
Shelled peanuts and peanut kernels	Blue jay, rufous-sided towhee, tufted titmouse, white throated sparrow
Safflower seeds	Cardinal
White proso millet	Fox sparrow, house finch, house sparrow, mourning dove, pine siskin, red-winged blackbird, white-crowned sparrow, white-throated sparrow
Chopped apples, pears and grapes; whole raisins, blueberries, currants	Insect-eating birds who stay throughout winter: American robin, bluebird, brown thrasher, eastern phoebe, gray catbird, mockingbird, northern oriole

pine siskin

tufted titmouse

red-winged blackbird

house finch

KEEP A "GUEST BOOK" FOR WILDLIFE VISITORS

Almost nothing adds as much to the enjoyment of attracting wildlife as keeping a journal of what the critters do while they're visiting.

Some people, especially birdfeeding enthusiasts, see the gray squirrel as one of the most bothersome

Why keep a nature notebook? You'll find precious memories in these notebooks down the line; you'll gain insights into your visitors, and along the way you may even make a new or important observation about wildlife behavior.

You don't have to be a great writer. It's not even important to write in complete sentences. All you really need are notes to jog your memory of what you saw and wanted to remember. A wildlife observation journal is intended as a personal journey, to share with your family or anyone you think would enjoy it. Many journal keepers, once they get over their shyness about trying to draw, also find they enjoy including little sketches of what they see, right along with their writing.

Keep your journal and a working ink pen (markers tend to smudge and run if they get wet) in some safe place near your favorite window for watching your backyard wildlife. Don't set too many rules for what you include in your journal. Some basics that most journal keepers eventually find they want to record include date and time of observation, weather information at the time, the species involved and the behavior observed (particularly behavior that relates to elements of your habitat).

Here's an optional – but very useful –

Keeping an ongoing journal of your nature and wildlife observations and insights will help you learn about your backyard habitat.

tip for your nature notebook: Include an indexing system. This allows you to track information on species, plants and habitat features throughout all of your journals. Use index cards, which are easily expanded and altered. Make out a card for each plant species in your habitat, each wildlife species you observe and each additional habitat feature. On the appropriate card, list the date whenever you discuss that topic in your journal.

pests in the backyard habitat. But many of us welcome squirrels, enjoying their antics, offering them their own supplies of corn and seeds, and even their own specialized feeders.

FEBRUARY

REGION-BY-REGION CHECKLIST

ZONES 2 AND 3 Step up your feeding program for all wildlife – this can be a critical period for many species. Keep water sources open with a stock tank de-icer, birdbath heater, or frequent ice-breaking. Put your old Christmas tree up outdoors as a temporary shelter (see page 14). Walking on frozen grasses or groundcovers can damage or even kill your plants, so stay on paths and walkways. Don't let snow and ice build up on your trees and shrubs; shake it off as necessary. Start your tree and shrub pruning now.

ZONE 4 Follow the activity checklist for Zones 2 and 3.

ZONE 5 Follow the activity checklist for Zones 2 and 3. Begin repairs as needed on trellises, arbors and other supports for vines, shrubs and trees. If the ground isn't frozen, install new supports planned for this year.

ZONE 6 Follow the activity checklist for Zone 5.

ZONE 7 Follow the activity checklist for Zone 6. Remove old growth as desired from ornamental grasses. Hardier annuals like pansies and snapdragons can be sown outdoors late in the month.

ZONE 8 Apply compost or another balanced organic fertilizer to groundcovers and lawns. Remove old growth as desired from ornamental grasses. You can start seeds of flowering plants indoors now. Hardier annuals like pansies and snapdragons can be sown outdoors late in the month. At the end of the month, remove winter mulches. Plant new trees and shrubs, fertilize previously planted trees and shrubs, and prune older trees and shrubs as needed.

ZONE 9 Follow the activity checklist for Zone 8. If February brings extended dry periods, water as necessary. Plant hardier annuals and perennials outdoors, and begin hardening off plants that were started indoors earlier. All winter mulches can now be removed.

ZONES 10 AND 11 Follow the activity checklist for Zone 9.

MAKE YOUR OWN SUET FEEDER

Suet is an incredibly versatile and important winter food source for birds and other wildlife.
It can be used in bulk, just as it comes from the butcher shop, or formed into shapes.

To make the most basic suet feeder, simply jab a hunk of raw suet on a stick or drop it into a plastic mesh sack, such as the type fresh onions are sold in. Hang the sack from the bottom of a bird feeder or under a tree limb, and the birds will soon be clinging to it, pecking bits of suet from inside.

For a more attractive feeder, you'll need a section of tree limb, several inches in diameter. Drill several 1- to 2-inch diameter holes 1 inch deep into all sides in a scattered pattern. Pack raw suet into the holes, or pour in melted suet and allow it to dry or harden. Hanging the limb feeder for use by the birds is as simple as screwing a screw eye into one of the ends.

To use the limb feeder on the side of a tree or the pole holding your other feeders, just cut the limb in half lengthwise and drill the suet holes on the outside only. Attach the cut limb to the side of the tree or pole with a long nail, or wire them together.

Melted suet also is ideal for some unique feeders. Tie strings around pinecones and dip them into a pot of liquefied suet; allow them to cool and harden slightly. Repeat this operation twice more to get a thick coating of suet. Tie the strings to tree limbs or hang them under your other feeders. Small evergreen boughs, with their needles still in place, can be used as an alternative to pinecones.

Another special suet feeder can be made from half a coconut shell, from which all the coconut meat has been scraped out. Drill three holes through the shell in a triangular pattern, about ½ inch down from the edge. Tie equal lengths of cord through the holes, joining them 6 to 8 inches above the coconut shell. Fill the shell to the brim with melted suet and allow to harden. Use the cord to hang the feeder wherever you want.

Pinecones dipped in suet and hung outside for the birds can be real conversation pieces when guests come to visit.

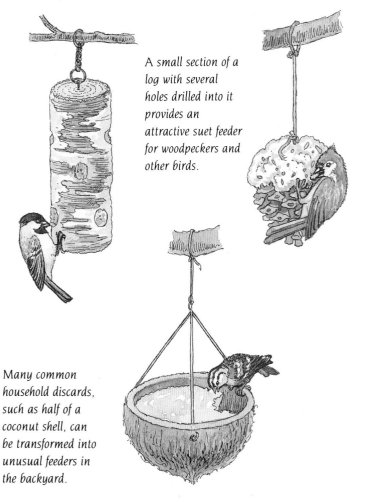

A small section of a log with several holes drilled into it provides an attractive suet feeder for woodpeckers and other birds.

Many common household discards, such as half of a coconut shell, can be transformed into unusual feeders in the backyard.

COMPOST INDOORS WITH EARTHWORMS

You can make compost year-round if you let earthworms do the work. Just set up a simple worm composting system in the basement.

To make a worm composter, start with a large container, anything from a plastic garbage can to a wooden box that you build yourself. Locate the container in the basement or another relatively cool, absolutely dark, out-of-the-way spot, where slight odors won't annoy anyone. The lid should fit tightly enough to keep flies out of the container but not so tightly that it cuts off all air. After all, both worms and compost have to breathe! It should be a solid lid to keep the light out and most moisture in.

Equip the container with a wire-mesh screen in a frame that fits snugly, above the bottom tenth of the container. Mark the spot on the container's side where the screen rests. Then remove the screen and fill the container up to the mark with irregularly shaped stones about 1 or 2 inches in diameter. Replace the screen over the stones and push it snugly into place, so that it leaves no gaps around the edges. This arrangement will provide a bit of drainage, just in case the moisture level in the container gets too high.

In the container, mix 2 parts well-composted leaf mulch that has been finely shredded, 2 parts sawdust, and 1 part soil from your backyard. (Some indoor-composting recipes suggest that you also add cow manure, but the resulting smell has put more than a few people off this whole concept.) Wet this mixture to damp-sponge consistency and let it sit for four or five days while it evens itself out.

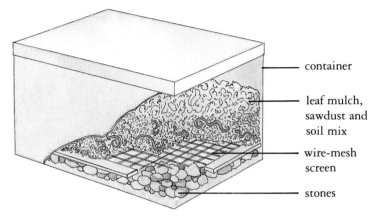

container

leaf mulch, sawdust and soil mix

wire-mesh screen

stones

Now add the worms

You can buy worms from a local bait shop or order them through garden supply catalogs. Look for red worms and brandling worms, since they don't mind the warm temperatures of the compost. You'll get a hardier stock if you dig up your own in the garden. You'll want smaller worms rather than the big guys that we call night crawlers. Start with three dozen in a 30-gallon container.

Feed them fruit and vegetable scraps from your kitchen, as well as bread, cooked pasta and rice and the like. (Yes, coffee grounds do make good worm food.) Don't include any meat products, since this can destroy the balance of the composting system. Put the scraps through a food processor or blender set on "chop" before spreading them across the surface of the mixture in the container. This will help the worms consume the scraps. You'll know you're feeding your worms too much if the food doesn't disappear within 24 hours.

A small indoor worm-powered composting system can keep your houseplants supplied with nutrients throughout the year.

The container's earthworm population will probably double every month or so. By the end of the second full month of operation, the original mix and added kitchen scraps will be thoroughly digested and transformed into some of the best compost you'll ever see. Now it's time to remove that compost for use in the garden, around the backyard, in planters or anywhere that could benefit from a compost boost. You can also thin your earthworm population back to the original level. Just sift through the compost with your fingers and remove 36 worms. Add the extra worms to your garden or yard.

Then you can start all over again with a fresh mix and three dozen worms.

A LOOK AT THE WOODCHUCK

February 2 is Groundhog Day in the United States. Traditionally, if the groundhog (woodchuck) sees its shadow, winter will last another six weeks, while no shadow means that spring is right around the corner.

Regardless of the truth in the groundhog's shadow legend, the emergence of the groundhog is a portent of approaching spring. February 2 is a rather arbitrary date, though, particularly in Canada and the northern reaches of the animal's range in the United States, where a much later date is more likely.

The widespread presence of the groundhog has provided a great deal of knowledge of the critter and tongue-in-cheek reinforcement of the notion. This small animal – a large male weighs maybe 15 pounds – is among the most common mammals. Its range extends as far west as Kansas, as far south as Alabama, north throughout all of the United States and north and west throughout much of Canada.

The groundhog's late-winter to early-spring emergence is a fearsome sight for the gardener, since one of the greatest gardening challenges is thwarting the voracious appetite of this persistent critter. (See page 17.) However, the groundhog in limited numbers has a beneficial impact on its environment. Its extensive burrowing breaks up and aerates the earth. Its feces, deposited in one specific chamber of the burrow network, provides rich fertilizer. (Imagine: woodchucks with bathrooms!) And the groundhog is an important part of the food chain. The woodchuck moniker is not related to any habits or habitats of this mammal but rather is derived from the name that Native Americans gave it. Their word *wuchak* was used interchangeably for several similar animals.

MOLE

Moles are hated by the lawn-loving fraternity across the country, primarily because of the tunnels that they dig through lawns. However, moles

are really performing a useful function, eating beetle grubs and other pests. And much of the damage to shrub and tree trunks blamed on moles is actually the work of other small rodents, such as voles and mice, that use mole paths.

KEEP WATER OPEN ALL WINTER

Keeping the water in the birdbath unfrozen has become an obsession for many people, as more and more of us have recognized its critical importance for wildlife during the winter months.

Wildlife needs water in winter. Many products, ranging from harmless solar-powered heaters to chemical anti-freeze solutions, which are lethal to wildlife, have come onto the market to fulfill this need. However, despite all these innovations and the claims of the marketers, the simplest and most effective method for combating the ice remains an electric heater unit.

You can choose from the specially designed birdbath heaters available through most nature and bird-supply stores. However, a much cheaper alternative is a basic aquarium heater, available through any pet shop.

Although plentiful snow and ice may lead us to think otherwise, finding open water is often difficult for birds and other critters during the frozen months of winter.

Installing a heater may sound like a major undertaking, but in fact the whole project can be completed in an hour or two with minimal disturbance of your landscape, no lasting visual or physical impact and a total cost somewhere in the neighborhood of a few deliveries from the local pizza shop.

Most people's number one objection in considering the electrical heater solution is the unsightly and obstacle-generating electrical cord coiling and bending across their lawn. So, let's move the whole affair underground. (This is normally a spring or summer project, when the soil isn't frozen, but I thought I'd be more likely to get your attention at this time of year.)

What you'll need

1½-inch-diameter plastic pipe, long enough to reach . . .
Connectors for the plastic pipe, if necessary
Pipe sealant
Heavy-duty, outdoor electrical cord, similar in length to plastic pipe plus some slack
Electrical tape
2 end caps to fit over the plastic pipe
Permanent glue

A heavy-duty electrical cord, encased in a buried plastic pipe, will provide ice-melting power at the bird bath.

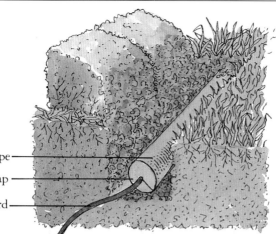

plastic pipe ———
end cap ———
electrical cord ———

Here's what to do

1 Use a spade to cut a trench from the electrical outlet to the birdbath. This trench needs to be no more than 1 foot deep. If you're digging it across open soil, simply place the soil on the opposite side of the trench. If you're digging it across lawn, lift blocks of sod by making a series of cuts: the first on your side of the trench, a second at right angles to the first across the width of the trench, and a third running parallel to the second. You now have three sides to a square. Do not cut the fourth side. Simply lift the block of sod and soil in one piece and, using the fourth side like a hinge, lay the block grass-side-down on the opposite side of the trench. When you've completed your digging, you will have a trench from the electrical outlet to the birdbath with all the blocks lined up on one side of the trench, still connected to the lawn.

2 Now, if you need more than one section of plastic pipe to reach the entire distance of the trench, use the connectors to attach the sections of pipe and apply sealant in and over all connections. You can do this on-site, laying the connected pipe along the side of the trench as you go.

3 Thread your electrical cord through the pipe. If you need more than one section of cord, splice the sections as you normally would, then wrap each connection with an ample covering of electrical tape. Cover the tape with generous amounts of sealant and allow the sealant to dry completely before threading the cord through the pipe.

4 Lay the pipe along the bottom of the trench and make certain that enough electrical cord extends out at either end to make the connection to both your electrical outlet and the cord on your birdbath heater.

5 With a sharp utility knife, cut from the side of each end cap to the center point of the end cap. At this center point, drill or cut a hole just large enough to accommodate the electrical cord. Insert the cord through the holes.

6 Repair the cuts you made in the end caps with permanent glue. Place one end cap over each end of the pipe, applying sealant inside and outside the connection. After the sealant has dried, check again to make sure there is adequate length of electrical cord extending out both ends of the pipe, then apply sealant in and around the holes in the end caps.

7 Replace the soil or sod-blocks over the pipe and stomp it down level with the rest of the soil or your lawn. If you were working in a lawn area, your blocks will soon reconnect to the neighboring soil, grass and roots.

8 By following these directions, you've created a fairly water-tight electrical line that you should try to keep dry when you connect your heater for winter use. Connect your electrical cord to the plug of your heater, and connect the electrical cord to the outlet. Wrap a plastic bag around the connection with the heater and seal it with ample electrical tape. If the outlet area doesn't already have some form of protection from the elements, buy and install one of the many designs available for just a few dollars in hardware stores and home centers.

SET UP A TEMPORARY BRUSH PILE

With the spread of suburbanization, brush piles have fallen out of favor. And that has meant the loss of an important habitat feature for wildlife.

In an earlier time, when more of us lived close to the land, brush piles were seen as a convenient place to stash branches and twigs after clearing the land or cutting firewood. They were an integral part of a landscape that supported wild creatures.

While your neighbors may not be inclined to overlook a brush pile in your suburban backyard throughout the year, they are generally less attentive to what's happening "out back" during the deep-winter months and more open to helping wildlife then. Your chances of bringing off a temporary brush pile without bringing on too much criticism are probably better in winter than at any other time of the year.

There are two key elements to any brush pile: height and covering. Height is easy – just pile on a few logs. You can make a simple covering with a few layers of evergreen boughs. In this example, you'll build a brush pile with outside dimensions of about 6½ feet in width, 5 feet in length and 3 feet in height.

What you'll need

15 logs, 5 feet long × 6 inches in diameter
Evergreen boughs
4 poles, 4 feet long × 1 inch in diameter
Heavy-gauge wire
Heavy-duty cord

Here's what to do

❶ Begin by laying five of the logs on the ground parallel to each other, spaced about a foot apart, with the two outermost logs lying about 6½ feet apart. The sides of the logs should be placed facing into the general direction from which your winter wind usually blows, leaving the openings between the logs at right angles to the wind.

❷ To hold the entire brush pile together, drive the poles into the ground on the outside of the outermost logs near either end. Drive the poles about a foot into the ground, leaving about 3 feet aboveground.

❸ Place a layer of freshly cut evergreen boughs across the top of the logs to a thickness of about 4 inches. The entire surface of the logs should be covered.

④ Lay five more logs across the top of the evergreens, at right angles to the first layer of logs and similarly spaced. The outermost logs of this layer should be laid immediately outside the poles you drove into the ground. Using heavy-gauge wire, bind these outer logs to the poles at all four corners.

shelter, toss a couple of handfuls of bird feed into the spaces between the bottom logs.

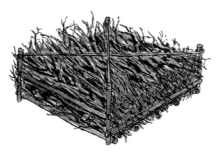

⑦ When winter has passed and you want to remove this temporary shelter, simply dismantle it layer by layer and run the materials through a chipper-shredder for a pile of nicely weathered wood-chip mulch. Of course, if your neighbors are tolerant, you can leave this same brush pile in place throughout the year. It will remain stable for several years, requiring only the addition of some new evergreen boughs before each winter.

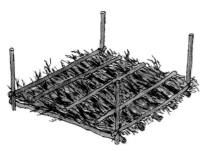

⑤ Repeat the above process, adding a second layer of evergreens, a third course of logs, and then a third layer of evergreens to a depth of about 8 inches (twice the original depth).

⑥ Tie a heavy cord across the top layer of evergreen boughs in an X from corner pole to corner pole, and snug it down tightly. Your brush pile is now ready for use by wildlife. To encourage quick acceptance of this new

The trimmings and cuttings from your backyard shrubs and trees make fine additions to your brush piles.

MARCH

REGION-BY-REGION CHECKLIST

ZONES 2 AND 3 Continue your feeding program for all wildlife. Keep your water sources open with a stock tank de-icer, birdbath heater, or frequent ice-breaking. You can start seeds indoors now to get a head start on vegetables and flowers this spring and summer. Apply compost or organic fertilizer around trees and shrubs.

ZONE 4 Some birds are already preparing their nests and will accept nesting materials like straw and yarn that you set out for them. Toward the end of the month, begin to gradually remove your winter mulches. Start seeds indoors for earlier flowers and vegetables. Prune trees and shrubs.

ZONE 5 Cut back ornamental grasses before they start new growth. Apply compost or another complete organic fertilizer to lawn, ornamental grasses, groundcovers and perennials. Sow hardy annuals outdoors. Continue to remove your winter mulches. Prune trees and shrubs, and apply organic fertilizer.

ZONE 6 Cut back ornamental grasses before they start new growth. Apply compost or another complete organic fertilizer to lawn, ornamental grasses, groundcovers and perennials. Sow hardy annuals outdoors. Start to prepare new beds and other planting areas. Continue to remove winter mulches. Prune summer- and fall-blooming trees and shrubs.

ZONE 7 Follow the activity checklist for Zone 6. Set out hummingbird feeders.

ZONE 8 Plant new perennials and divide established ones as needed. Deadhead (cut off) perennial blooms when they fade. Prune hedges and specimen shrubs. Apply compost or another balanced organic fertilizer to trees, shrubs and vines. Get your hummingbird feeders into operation.

ZONE 9 Follow the activity checklist for Zone 8. Prune spring-blooming trees and shrubs when flowering is finished.

ZONES 10 AND 11 Follow the activity checklist for Zone 9.

TAKE BETTER WILDLIFE PHOTOS

Once you start attracting wildlife to your yard,

you'll want to capture them on film.

The best way to get better photos of your backyard wildlife is to put some distance between yourself and the critters, and press the shutter button from the comfort of your home.

The easiest, if not the cheapest, way to take those photos you admire in the magazines is with a 35-mm single-lens-reflex (SLR) camera that accepts interchangeable lenses and a 300-mm lens. That's the way the pros do it.

If the price tag for that 35-mm setup – mid to high three figures for even the most basic equipment – is out of the question, there are photographic products available at most camera stores that can do much the same thing at much less expense. They're called cable releases. For a few hundred dollars, you can have a radio-controlled cable release that can cover just about any backyard distance. And if that's still too pricey, there are pneumatic-bulb-controlled releases that connect to the shutter button of your camera by means of a cable and let you operate the camera from 20 or 30 feet away. These generally sell for less than $50.

With any of these setups, you can use your home as a hiding place. Either set up a 35-mm SLR with a long lens by a convenient open window, or set up your camera within a few feet of where you expect to see the critter, connect the cable to the shutter button, and lead the cable from the camera back to the house and in through the window.

The least expensive method requires a bit more patience, luck and practice to produce great shots than just looking through the camera and pushing the shutter button when you have the critter framed just the way you want it. Keep trying and don't get discouraged – it *can* be done with patience, practice and lots of film.

When looking for prime wildlife photography opportunities, don't overlook the most convenient spots for observation, such as windows in your home that overlook feeding areas and sources of water that you've established in your backyard habitat to attract birds and other wildlife.

START WILDFLOWER SEEDS INDOORS

Most wildflower seeds will do just fine when planted. However, there are some good reasons
why you might want to start at least some of your wildflowers indoors.

Starting wildflowers indoors can extend their flowering period by months. In the north, this season-stretching can make the use of a wider variety of wildflowers possible. In addition, starting seeds indoors under controlled conditions will produce the most reliable germination.

Perhaps the best decision for most gardeners is to jump-start a small amount of the seed for any given species indoors and save most of the seeds in a water-tight, airtight, light-proof container for later planting outdoors.

You can buy commercial growing mixes, but they may contain chemical fertilizers. Check the label before you buy. Or, with a little more effort, you can prepare your own mix.

Here's what to do

❶ First you need to sterilize some soil gathered from the site where you intend to transplant the young plants outdoors. Spread a couple of trowelfuls of soil onto a foil-covered cookie sheet, smoothing the soil to a depth of about 1 inch. Cover the soil with another sheet of foil, folding the edges under the cookie sheet. Put the cookie sheet into an oven pre-heated to

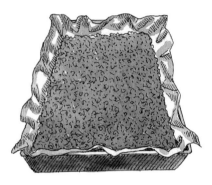

200°F. Bake for 30 minutes. Remove the soil from the oven and allow it to cool completely. Then force it through a sifter to give it a fine, loose texture. Remove any lumps that will not break down.

❷ Gather a couple of trowelfuls of well-composted leaf mold and shred it into tiny bits and strips. Mix one part of sterilized soil with one part of shredded leaf mold and and press the mixture through a sieve. Thoroughly combine the soil and leaf mold mix with coarse sand at a ratio of two to one.

❸ Spoon the mixture into pots, cell-packs or flats to within an inch of the top. Add a layer of vermiculite or perlite on top of your mixture to within ¼ inch of the top of each pot. This top layer will allow the

seeds to sprout easily. They can then spread their roots into the denser soil mix below.

❹ Place a layer of pebbles (from an aquarium supply shop or a freshwater stream) in the bottom of the tray in which your pots of seed will stand. This will prevent the accumulation of water in your growing medium. Wash them thoroughly with clean water.

❺ Make sure the planting medium is moist but not dripping wet. Dribble just a few seeds over the surface of each pot. In a 1-inch-square planting cell, sow just 3 or 4 well-spaced seeds. In a 5-inch-diameter pot, sow only 20 or so well-spaced seeds. Such precise sowing may require you to place a few of the

seeds onto a small piece of paper and then push them off individually with a toothpick. You don't want the seeds to sprout in thick clusters, because when the small plants emerge you'll need to thin them to about one per square inch.

6 Top the seeds with no more than a ⅛-inch layer of sphagnum moss that you rub through a sieve into place over the seeds. The depth of this layer is critical. It absolutely must not be more than ⅛ inch. Wildflower seeds have evolved to germinate without any tilling of the soil. In the wild, they simply fall to the ground and struggle to take hold where they land. The biggest mistake gardeners make when starting wildflowers – indoors or outdoors – is to sow the seeds in too deeply. In general this prevents the seeds from germinating. Label every pot with the species and variety or cultivar it contains.

7 Stand the pots on the tray of pebbles and gently mist the tops of the pots with water. Add water to the tray, just enough to come up over the bottoms of the pots. Then enclose the entire tray, pots and all, in a plastic bag or cover the pots with a piece of glass. If you know the light-germination requirements of the species you're working with, place the trays in darkness or under fluorescent lights as required. Otherwise, place the tray in a dark, warm location.

8 Check the tray daily, making certain the growing medium has not dried out. As soon as the seedlings show, remove the plastic bag or glass and move the tray under fluorescent lights, with the tops of the plants about 4 inches below the lights. Leave the lights on for 12 to 16 hours per day. (If after 10 or 12 days the seeds have not germinated, move the tray under the lights and proceed as described above.)

9 When the seedlings have their first true leaves, use straight-bladed cuticle scissors to cut off all but one plant per square inch, being careful not to even brush against the plant to be left behind.

As the young plants grow, gradually increase the space between their top leaves and the lights to about 10 inches and then maintain that distance.

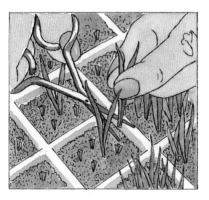

10 Place the pots or cells into room-temperature water, an inch or so deep, whenever the seedlings show any sign of drying out, such as when the surface of the medium is dry, or

when the pot feels lighter than usual. As soon as the surface of the growing medium feels moist to the touch, remove the pots or cells, give them a few minutes for any excess water to drain off, and then return them to the tray.

11 After the young plants have sprouted a set or two of true leaves, they are ready for transplanting into larger pots – one plant per 2 square inches – with the same growing medium you started them in. Use a teaspoon to lift the seedlings without disturbing their roots, and transfer the whole root ball into the new pot. Gently smooth the growing medium in around that root ball, and avoid touching the stem.

12 When you're ready to move the plants outdoors, do it gradually and gently by hardening them off first. Here's how: Beginning with a few hours under a shaded covering, increase the time the plants spend outdoors over a period of ten days. When they show signs of new growth, remove the covering and water the plants with fish emulsion or seaweed concentrate. A few days later they'll be ready to transplant into their ultimate location. Do all outdoor transplanting on overcast days or in the early morning or late afternoon.

BUILD UNIQUE NESTBOXES

Here are some great nestbox ideas for your backyard. You can tailor them to suit the needs

of the species you want to attract by checking "Nestbox Specs" before

constructing your nestbox.

Rustic nestbox

You can make an unusual, natural-looking nestbox that will be very attractive to woodland nesters, such as nuthatches and titmice, using the trunk of a tree as the primary raw material.

What you'll need

Section of solid tree trunk,
    9 inches long × 6 inches in
    diameter
12 × 6 × ¾-inch exterior
    plywood
18 × 5 × 1-inch rough-cut board
    with bark intact
Ten 1¾-inch wood screws
Six 2½-inch wood screws

Here's what to do

1 Start with a section of trunk from a solid (not hollow) tree — birch and pine are excellent for this project. Saw each end of the trunk section to produce flat surfaces. Mark which end of the trunk section will be the top of your nestbox.

2 Trace both ends of the trunk on the plywood, and label the top section. Cut the two traced circles from the plywood with a jigsaw.

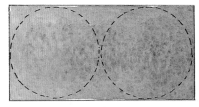

3 Cut lengthwise through the middle of the trunk section, producing two relatively equal semicircular halves. Using a hammer and chisel, remove the wood from the center of each half, creating a circular hollow roughly 4 inches in diameter in the center when you hold the two pieces together.

4 Attach one of your two trunk halves to the rough-cut board, bark side to bark side, leaving 3 inches of the board extending above the trunk half and 6 inches extending below it. Attach the trunk to the board with 1¾-inch wood screws with 3 spaced evenly above and 3 spaced evenly below.

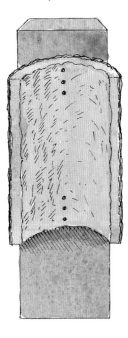

5 Drill a 1¼-inch entrance hole centered 2 inches from the top of the second trunk half all the way through the wood. Rejoin the two trunk halves with 2½-inch wood screws. Drill four holes; two on either side of the entrance hole, 3

inches from the top and 3 inches from the bottom. Drive the wood screws through those holes.

6 Drill several small drainage holes through the plywood circle intended for the bottom of the nestbox. Then, attach the top and bottom circles of plywood to the rejoined trunk with four 1¾-inch wood screws through each circle.

7 To mount the nestbox to the side of a tree or pole, simply drive 2½-inch wood screws through the board areas that extend above and below the nestbox into the tree or pole.

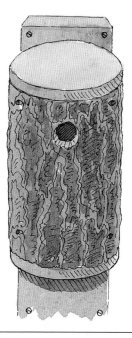

Birdhouse gourd

Another unusual nestbox can be made from a strange-looking gourd that is showing up more and more at farmers' markets and roadside stands across much of the country. Alternatively, if you want to grow your own gourds, gardening catalogs now offer seeds for something called a birdhouse gourd (*Langenaria siceraria*). These gourds are the same type once grown by Native Americans and prepared as birdhouses to attract purple martins to their fields, where the birds consumed great numbers of insects.

Make sure the gourd you use has dried completely. Then drill an entrance hole into one of the sides of the large hollow part of the gourd – for size, refer to "Nestbox specs" on page 38. Also drill a few small drainage holes into what will be the bottom of the nestbox. Apply a couple of coats of clear varnish. Hang the gourd by the remaining bit of stem or by drilling holes through the end.

The very first nestboxes in America were the birdhouse gourds made by native Americans.

NESTBOX SPECS

Species	Floor (inches)	Depth (inches)	Entrance above floor (inches)	Entrance diameter (inches)	Height above ground (feet)
American kestrel	11 × 11	12	9–12	3 × 4	20–30
American robin	6 × 8	8	no sides		6–15
Barn owl	10 × 18	15–18	4	6	12–18
Barn swallow	6 × 6	6	no sides		8–12
Black-capped chickadee	4 × 4	8–10	6–8	1⅛	6–15
Carolina wren	4 × 4	6–8	1–6	1½	6–10
Common flicker	7 × 7	16–18	14–16	2½	6–20
Crested flycatcher	6 × 6	8	6	2	8–20
Downy woodpecker	4 × 4	9–12	6–8	1¼	6–20
Eastern bluebird	5 × 5	8	6	1½	5
Eastern screech owl	8 × 8	12–15	9–12	3	10–30
European starling	6 × 6	16–18	14–16	2	10–25
Hairy woodpecker	6 × 6	12–15	9–12	1½	12–20
House finch	6 × 6	6	4	2	6–12
House wren	4 × 4	8–10	1–6	1¼	6–10
Purple martin	6 × 6	6	1	2½	10–20
Red-headed woodpecker	6 × 6	12	10	2	10–20
Song sparrow	6 × 6	6	no sides		1–3
Tree swallow	5 × 5	6–8	5–6	1½	6–16
Tufted titmouse	4 × 4	8–10	6–8	1¼	6–15
White-breasted nuthatch	4 × 4	8–10	6–8	1¼	12–20
Wood duck	10 × 18	10–24	12–16	4	10–20

PROTECT BIRDS FROM WINDOWS

If bird-and-window collisions are a regular problem in your backyard habitat,
it's time to take a look at the situation from the birds' perspective.

Birds don't understand windows. To them, our panes of glass generally appear to be one of two things: a passageway through which they can fly, or (as a reflection) a rival bird of their own species that mocks and mimics every movement they make. Either way, the bird's encounter with a window is not a positive one. The luckier birds find themselves knocked to the ground and stunned temporarily. Many others, however, meet death against the glass.

Take a look at your windows

Go out to your feeders, birdbaths, perching areas and other spots that attract birds, and look back at your windows from these perspectives. Do any of the windows have the appearance of a passageway? Can you see the outdoors on the far side of your house right through any of the windows? Do you see blue sky? It's never just the fact that a window exists that causes the problem. It's always a combination of factors, such as the line of sight between a window and a birdfeeder. Look for all possible factors before deciding on a course of action.

Consider the options

With your evaluation of the true causes of the collisions complete, you're ready to consider several options to remedy the situation. You can:
• Keep the curtains drawn to eliminate the optical illusion of an open passageway;

• Hang strips of paper or ribbons in front of the window on the outside;
• Apply decals to the window to make the glass look more like a barrier;
• Apply a silhouette decal of a hawk in flight to the window to warn off the birds;
• Move the feeder or birdbath to eliminate the line of sight that's causing the problem;
• Plant a tree or tall shrub between the window and the feeder or birdbath to break flight path and reflection.

Dealing with an accident

Those birds that hit the glass and are found stunned, but not killed, on the ground below the window generally will recover from the incident relatively quickly. Place them in some warm, dry, protected location and leave them to their own devices.

If a bird dies, be aware that, without proper permits, it's generally illegal for the average person to possess any portion of a protected bird, even a single feather. However, your local high school or university biology department, nature center, wildlife agency office or museum probably has the necessary permits and might appreciate the offer of certain specimens. (Call ahead to determine if they want the bird and how they want it delivered. You may not legally transport it yourself.) Otherwise, move the bird to your brush pile or other secluded spot and let nature take its course.

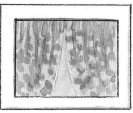
keep curtains drawn

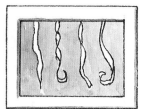
ribbons or strips of paper

hawk decals

APRIL

REGION-BY-REGION CHECKLIST

ZONES 2 AND 3 Many species of birds are preparing their nests and will accept nesting materials like straw and yarn if you set them out. Gradually remove your winter mulches. Divide your summer-blooming perennials. Prune pines, firs, spruces and other conifers as needed.

ZONE 4 Nesting season is gearing up now. Sow new lawns. Plant ornamental grasses and groundcovers. Divide summer-blooming perennials. Prune pines, firs, spruces and other conifers. Apply compost or another balanced organic fertilizer to trees and shrubs.

ZONE 5 Follow the activity checklist for Zone 4. Apply compost or another balanced organic fertilizer to established perennials, trees, shrubs and vines.

ZONE 6 Nesting season is under way. Sow new lawns, plant ornamental grasses and groundcovers, and apply compost or another balanced organic fertilizer. Plant new perennials and divide those that have already bloomed. You'll notice a wider variety of insects this month.

ZONE 7 Follow the activity checklist for Zone 6. Plant hardy annuals like pansies and snapdragons outdoors. Plant new trees, shrubs and vines, and apply compost or another balanced organic fertilizer to them. Prune spring-blooming trees and shrubs when they finish flowering.

ZONE 8 Nesting season is in full swing now. Plant new groundcovers. Apply compost or another balanced organic fertilizer to lawns, ornamental grasses, groundcovers, perennials and annuals. Mulch your perennial beds to reduce weeds and conserve moisture. Sow or set transplants of hardy annuals outdoors. Prune spring-blooming shrubs after they have finished flowering. Prune hedges and thickets as needed. Keep the lawnmower blade set high.

ZONE 9 Follow the activity checklist for Zone 8. Pull out winter annuals and compost them.

ZONES 10 AND 11 Follow the activity checklist for Zone 9.

RESCUING WILDLIFE: WHEN DO YOU NEED TO?

More often than not, that seemingly helpless little orphaned creature abandoned in your backyard is neither orphaned nor abandoned.

What should you do if you find a baby bird or other creature? If you don't see a dead adult or dead littermates nearby; if the little creature isn't cold, wet or limp; and if it's not in any immediate danger, let it be. Keep it under watch and check on it closely again three or four hours later. If it's still there and its condition doesn't appear to have deteriorated from the last time you saw it, let it be. (Chances are, it will be gone.) Keep it under watch and check on it closely again three or four hours later. Only when any of these conditions change or after several close checks should you consider intervention.

What should you do?

Your first phase of intervention should be an all-out attempt to return the little critter to its nest, which should be relatively close at hand if the baby is truly as helpless as you think it is. If the nest can't be located or is out of reach, create a substitute nest from a plastic strawberry carton or small box, fill it with tissue and place it securely in an appropriate location, such as the highest crook of a limb you can reach (for a baby bird) or a weedy area (for a baby rabbit). The spot should be sheltered from the sun and rain by something like an overhanging branch. Check on the youngster a few hours later, paying close attention to the same points listed above.

Even if the adult does not show up within what you feel is an acceptable amount of time, and realistically that may be most of a day, you probably should not take on the responsibility of caring for the orphaned critter yourself – it is more than most of us can handle. Many very young animals need almost constant attention and help with almost every aspect of their lives, from proper food on a round-the-clock schedule to assistance in eliminating wastes.

Far better than taking on such responsibilities is to spend your time in a realistic attempt to help the critter. Locate the nearest wildlife rehabilitator or rescuer and get the baby into their experienced hands. Your state wildlife agency, which is listed in the Yellow Pages, can quickly supply you with the name and number.

These nestling song sparrows obviously are not abandoned or in need of any human help. Even in less obvious situations, young wild things are not necessarily abandoned just because we don't see the parents at a particular moment. A wait-and-see approach is usually the best.

CREATE A WOODLAND GARDEN

These easy-going groundcovers will transform the bare soil beneath your trees into an almost magical flowering woodland garden and provide shelter for wildlife, too.

All of us would like to have a bit of woodland on our properties. But if you're lucky enough to have mature trees in your yard and have tried to grow lawn under them, you know how effectively a thick overstory of heavily leaved tree branches can cut out the light for plants below. The key to creating a lovely woodland garden is choosing shade-tolerant wildflowers and groundcovers.

The following selections will all grow and bloom beneath your trees. All of them provide thick shelter and cover. I've noted additional features that are attractive to wildlife.

Bunchberry (*Cornus canadensis*) does best in partial shade and moist, but well-drained slightly acid soil. It grows 2 to 6 inches tall and spreads quickly by creeping roots. It's hardy in Zones 2 through 10. The tiny, light green flowers are encircled by four white bracts. The dogwood-like flowers are attractive to some nectar-eating insects, and the red berries that appear in fall are enjoyed by wildlife.

Coral bells (*Heuchera sanguinea*) enjoys partial shade and rich, well-drained soil. It grows 3 to 6 inches tall but is slow to spread. It is hardy in Zones 5 through 10. The sprays of small, pink or reddish, bell-shaped flowers, borne in early summer, attract butterflies.

bunchberry

David viburnum

daylily

Creeping mahonia (*Mahonia repens*) does equally well in partial or full shade and in rich, moist but well-drained, slightly acid soil. It grows up to 12 inches tall and spreads rapidly by root. It is hardy in Zones 6 through 10. It produces 1-inch-wide, yellow flowers in spring and purple or dark blue berries in fall. The berries attract wildlife.

Creeping phlox (*Phlox stolonifera*) adapts well to either partial or full shade and rich, moist, slightly acid soil. It grows up to 10 to 14 inches tall and spreads at a moderate pace. It is hardy in Zones 4 through 10. The white, rose or blue flowers are borne in mid-spring and attract many nectar-eating insects.

David viburnum (*Viburnum davidii*) enjoys partial to full shade and rich, moist, slightly acid soil. It grows 12 to 30 inches tall and spreads very slowly. It is hardy in Zones 7 through 10. Small, white, bell-shaped flowers are borne in midsummer and are followed by dark blue berries in fall, which are eaten by many species of birds.

Daylily (*Hemerocallis* spp.) does well in almost all light conditions, including partial shade, and is adaptable to a wide range of soil types in Zones 3 through 10. It grows 12 to 60 inches tall and spreads very quickly across almost any site. The showy funnel-shaped flowers can be orange, apricot, yellow, cream, red, purple, or a combination, depending on the cultivar. Each bloom lasts for just one day, but the plant continues to produce new flowers over a three- to four-week period in late spring and summer. For greatest wildlife attraction, particularly if you enjoy watching hummingbirds, choose cultivars with reddish flowers.

English primrose *(Primula vulgaris)* does well in partial shade and rich, moist, well-drained soil, spreading slowly by seed. It grows 4 to 6 inches tall and is hardy in Zones 5 through 8. Yellow flowers appear in late spring. They are attractive to butterflies and moths of many species.

Horned violet *(Viola cornuta)* thrives in partial to full shade and rich, moist, well-drained soil. It grows 6 to 12 inches tall and spreads quickly by seed. It is hardy in Zones 5 through 10 and produces purple or white flowers in late spring. Nectar attracts butterflies.

Meadow anemone *(Anemone canadensis)* does best in partial shade and moist, but well-drained, slightly acid soil. It grows 12 to 24 inches tall and self-sows readily. It is hardy in Zones 4 through 10. The 2-inch-wide white flowers with yellow stamens are borne in early summer. They attract many species of woodland butterflies and other insect-eating insects. The tiny seeds that eventually drop from the flower heads are eaten by birds and small mammals.

Partridgeberry *(Mitchella repens)* will grow in partial to full shade and rich, moist soil. It only grows 1 or 2 inches tall and usually gets off to a slow start, but then spreads quickly by rooting stems. It is hardy in Zones 4 through 10. The ½-inch-wide, pink or white,

English primrose

red lungwort

wintergreen

horned violet

funnel-shaped flowers are borne in late spring. The red berries, which are a diet staple for many species of wildlife, appear from late summer into fall.

Red lungwort *(Pulmonaria rubra)* prefers partial to full shade and rich, moist soil. It grows up to 16 inches tall and spreads at a moderate rate by both creeping roots and seeds. It is hardy in Zones 4 through 8. It produces ¾-inch-wide, deep red flowers in hanging clusters in summer. These are particularly attractive to hummingbirds.

Two-row sedum *(Sedum spurium)* is a plant of partial shade and rich, moist, well-drained soil and spreads quickly by trailing stems. It is hardy in Zones 3 through 10. It produces white or pink starry flowers that are ½-inch wide and are borne in clusters in mid- to late-summer. The flowers are attractive to hummingbirds and insect-eating insects. The leaves turn red in winter.

Wintergreen *(Gaultheria procumbens)* grows best in partial shade and moist, well-drained, slightly acid soil. It grows 6 to 12 inches tall and spreads quickly by creeping roots. It is hardy in Zones 5 through 10 and produces white, bell-shaped flowers from late spring to early summer. The red berries that appear in early- to mid-fall are the most attractive part of the plant to wildlife.

Woolly blue violet *(Viola sororia)* will grow in partial to full shade but needs protection from the afternoon sun. It grows in rich, moist, well-drained soil, reaching 18 to 24 inches tall, and spreads quickly from seed. It is hardy in Zones 5 through 10. The clusters of ½-inch-wide, dark flowers attract butterflies in early spring.

DEVELOP A SMALL-SCALE WILDFLOWER MEADOW

No matter how small your yard is, you can plant a mini-meadow overflowing with colorful wildflowers, native grasses and, of course birds, butterflies and other wildlife.

A key to developing a backyard wildflower area that will have the look and feel of a real meadow lies in site selection. It should, of course, blend in well with the rest of the property, both plants and buildings. But, to create the real feel of a wildflower meadow, it must also look natural and unstructured.

The easiest way to get this natural look is by taking advantage of any slopes, curves or bends that are already on your property. If you're fortunate enough to have a small, but noticeable knoll or hill, consider siting your meadow on one or more of its sides. Wherever you site your meadow, don't choose a simple circle, oval, square or rectangle when preparing your planting area. An S shape, a comma, an angled lightning bolt or other irregular pattern will give the natural look most meadow gardeners are searching for.

Regardless of size, you'll enjoy nearly any meadow planting more if you create some sort of pathway leading into or through it. Take a close look at a wild meadow near your home. Many wildlife trails and small openings, which may be missed when viewing the meadow from a distance, soon become evident on more detailed examination. Not only will a path make it easier to get into your meadow, it will make it easier to work there, too.

First, prepare the site

Preparation of the site before planting is critical to the success of a new wildflower area, You should prepare for a meadow like you would for a new lawn. In early spring, mark the general outline of the meadow with some easily seen, but biodegradable, material like ground limestone or flour from the

A beautiful wildflower meadow can be added to nearly any backyard, regardless of the space available. You'll enjoy the colorful flowers as well as the butterflies, birds and other critters that come to visit or make their home there. No matter how small your meadow is, design creativity can give an illusion of much grander spaces.

Many different insects are lumped together under the name "bee", including everything from the relatively docile bumblebee to the aggressive yellow-jacket. All of them are feared and

disliked by many people because of the aggressive nature of a few like the yellow-jacket. Don't be a bee bigot!

kitchen. This will also give you the chance to step back and determine if you really have the shape that you want. Erasing and redrawing is easy at this point.

Once you have decided on your outline, dig along the line with a shovel or spade to a depth of about 8 inches, depositing the soil inside the outline. This stage is complete when you have a trench around the entire area. Now, rotary-till the area planned for planting to a depth of about 8 inches.

Plant the entire area with a cover crop of buckwheat, sown so thickly that it will smother any competition from weeds. (You can buy buckwheat seed through mail order seed companies or farm supply stores.) Before this crop of buckwheat flowers and is able to set seed, till it back into the soil and plant a second crop of the same. Again, before the buckwheat flowers, till it back into the soil.

Now plant your meadow

By the time you've tilled in the second buckwheat crop, it will be fall. Your meadow area will be weed-free and ready to burst with organically rich soil. You can plant your meadow now or the following spring. (Consult the instructions for the seeds you have chosen for the seed company's recommendation as to when to plant, or check in one of the wildflower meadow books in "Recommended Reading" on page 157.) Select suitable plants using "Wildflowers for all regions" on page 46.

Rake the soil to a smooth consistency. If you are planting now, mix your wildflower seeds with damp sawdust or sand and scatter the mixture over the site. Tamp the mixture into place very lightly, and cover the area with a very thin mulch of oat, wheat or pine straw. (You should be able to see the soil through the straw.) If you're waiting until spring, cover the site with a very thick layer of mulch that will prevent the growth of just about everything on the site, such as weed-free straw, or use black plastic. Then, shortly before you're ready to plant in the spring, remove the mulch and proceed as described above.

WILDFLOWERS FOR ALL REGIONS

When you select wildflowers and grasses, make sure the species you choose are well adapted to your region.

For the Northeast

Wildflowers: Asters, including azure aster and New England aster, baptisia, bee balm, black-eyed Susans, blazing-stars, blue-eyed grass, blue phlox, boneset, butterfly weed, cardinal flower, columbine, common milkweed and swamp milkweed, evening primrose, goldenrods, including sweet goldenrod, ironweeds, including New York ironweed, Joe-Pye weeds, lance-leaved coreopsis, long-plumed purple avens, lupine, penstemons, purple coneflower, shooting-star, sneezeweed, spiderwort, spring beauty, sunflowers, including swamp sunflower, tickseed sunflower, wild bergamot, wild cranesbill and yarrow.

Native grasses: Broom sedge, June grass, little bluestem, meadow fescue, side oats gramma, switch grass and wild oats.

For the Southeast

Wildflowers: Asters, including calico aster, New England aster and smooth aster, baptisia, bee balm, black-eyed Susans, blanket flower, blazingstars, including rough blazingstar, blue-eyed grass, blue phlox, boneset, butterfly weed, columbine, common milkweed and swamp milkweed, coneflower, dwarf-crested iris, evening primrose, fireweed, goldenrods, including seaside goldenrod, ironweeds, including New York ironweed, Joe-Pye weeds, lance-leaved coreopsis, lupine, martagon lily, penstemons, purple coneflower,

sneezeweed

black-eyed Susan

switch grass

shooting-star, sneezeweed, spiderwort, spring beauty, larkspur, Stokes' aster, sunflowers, including swamp sunflower, tickseed sunflower, trout lily, wild bergamot, wild cranesbill and white wild indigo.

Native grasses: Asian grass, broom sedge, little bluestem, sheep's fescue, switch grass and zebra grass

For the Midwest

Wildflowers: Asters, including azure aster, New England aster and smooth aster, baptisia, black-eyed Susans, blazingstar, bluebell, blue flax, blue phlox, butterfly weed, columbine, common milkweed and swamp milkweed, coneflowers, including prairie coneflower, evening primrose, goldenrods, including sweet goldenrod, ironweeds, including western ironweeds, lance-leaved coreopsis, lupine, penstemons, purple coneflower, purple prairie clover, shooting-star, sneezeweed, spiderwort, spring beauty, sundrops, sunflowers, including swamp sunflower, tickseed sunflower, trout lily, western phlox, wild bergamot and wild cranesbill.

Native grasses: Big bluestem, Indian grass, needle-and-thread grass, side oats gramma and switch grass.

For the West

Wildflowers: Alumroot, anemone, beach sundrops, bluebell and desert bluebell, blue columbine, golden columbine, yellow columbine and scarlet columbine, blue flag iris and tough-leaf iris, blue flax, butterfly weed, California poppy, chocolate lily, coastal lily, gumbo lily, trout lily and wood lily, Columbia clematis, cutleaf fleabane and daisy fleabane, deerhorn clarkia, delphinium, dotted blazingstar, evening primrose, including tufted evening primrose, fireweed, goldenrods, penstemon, including Cascade penstemon and scarlet bugler, hoary vervain, larkspur, long-plumed purple avens, monkey flower, prairie aster, prairie coneflower, silky phacelia, sneezeweed, spring beauty, sulphur flower, sunflowers, western shooting-star and yellow bell.

Native grasses: Big bluestem, buffalo grass, Indian grass, little bluestem and side oats gramma.

For the Southwest

Wildflowers: Baby-blue-eyes, blanket flower, blazingstar, blue columbine and scarlet columbine, blue-eyed grass, blue thimble flower, butterfly weed, California poppy, calliopsis, Chinese-houses, coneflowers, including prairie coneflower, desert bluebell, evening primrose, farewell-to-spring, fireweed, fivespot, golden lupine and arroyo lupine, gumbo lily, hoary vervain, lance-leaved coreopsis, little golden zinnia, long-plumed purple avens, meadow goldenrod and narrow goldenrod, mountain phlox, prairie aster, purple prairie clover, sneezeweed, sulphur flower, sunset flower, swamp milkweed, tansy phacelia, tidy tips, white evening primrose, wild four-o'clocks and yellow bell.

Native grasses: Blue gramma, buffalo grass and Indian rice grass.

For the Northwest

Wildflowers: Baby-blue-eyes, blanket flower, bluebell, birds' eye gilia, blue-eyed grass, blue flax, blue thimble flower, California goldenrod, California poppy, calliopsis, camass, Chinese-houses, daisy fleabane, farewell-to-spring, fireweed, fivespot, golden lupine, long-plumed purple avens, mountain phlox, red ribbons, sneezeweed, spring beauty, sunflowers, trout lily, tough-leaf iris, western shooting-star, wild sweet william, wind poppy and yellow bell.

Native grasses: Big bluestem and little bluestem.

These blanket flowers in a northeast wildflower planting are not the result of mere chance. Matching a wildflower species to its region almost always increases planting success.

PLANT SPECIAL HEDGES FOR WILDLIFE

Hollies and viburnums make dense hedges as well as provide a profusion of wildlife-attracting berries and protective cover.

Usually a light touch is better in the backyard wildlife habitat, but to produce the truly dense growth needed for a hedge, these broadleaved deciduous and evergreen shrubs require annual and heavy pruning. A more formally pruned hedge is actually better for wildlife from a shelter and cover standpoint. With hollies (*Ilex* spp.), until the hedge reaches the desired height, remove at least a third of each year's new shoots all around the sides. With viburnums (*Viburnum* spp.) prune the oldest few branches annually after the bloom has passed. This will prevent the production of a bare, treelike base.

Additionally, the trick to getting a good berry crop on your hollies is to have both male and female plants in your hedge: this is mostly a family of dioecious plants, meaning that each plant is of one sex. With viburnums, berry production is generally improved when several different cultivars are planted together so they can cross-pollinate one another.

The perfect shrub for a hedge not only provides dense, protective cover and shelter, but also an abundant source of fruit, nuts or berries through the lean winter months. Here a white-throated sparrow feeds on a winterberry holly.

Selected hollies (*Ilex* spp.)
The following species are among the more cold-hardy hollies:

American holly (*I. opaca*) can grow as tall as 35 feet in the home landscape, but it's slow-growing and will remain at hedge level for many years. The leaves are dark green on top and yellow-green underneath. The berries are dull red. Zones 5–9.

Blue holly (*I. × meserveae*) has a definite bluish tint to its leaves and stems, accented beautifully by bright red berries. Choose a compact cultivar, since taller blue hollies will eventually reach 15 to 20 feet. Zones 4–8.

Chinese holly (*I. cornuta*) produces dense and rounded growth of shiny green leaves and long-lasting bright red berries. Choose a compact cultivar unless you want a tall hedge, since taller Chinese hollies will grow to 10 feet. Zones 7–9.

Japanese holly (*I. crenata*) produces a very dense growth of dark green, fine-textured leaves and inconspicuous black berries. Many cultivars are compact and low-growing, forming an attractive alternative to dwarf boxwood (which Japanese holly resembles) and ground-covering junipers. Zones 6–9.

Winterberry (*I. verticillata*) will drop its leaves in the fall, but this native of the swamps is a good choice for low-lying, wet areas. The leaves are bright green, and the berries are bright red. Choose a cultivar like 'Winter Red' or 'Sparkleberry' that's noted for heavy fruiting – and don't forget to plant a male pollinator! Zones 4–9.

Yaupon holly (*I. vomitoria*) is a native of the southeastern United States. The evergreen leaves are bright green, and the berries are bright red. Plants eventually reach 15 to 25 feet tall, so choose a tower-growing cultivar. Zones 7–9.

Selected viburnums (*Viburnum* spp.)
Although most viburnums are deciduous north of Zone 7, they do produce dense cover and shelter and plentiful berry crops.

American cranberrybush viburnum (*V. trilobum*) is a large (8–12 foot) deciduous shrub with bright green maplelike leaves, 4-inch-wide white flower clusters, and scarlet berries that last well into winter. Zones 3–7.

Burkwood viburnum (*V. × burkwoodii*) is a hybrid that remains semi-evergreen as far north as Zone 4 and is evergreen in the South. It produces dark green leaves, fragrant white flowers in 3-inch clusters and red fruits that mature to black. Plants can reach 6 feet tall. Zones 4–8.

'Eve Price' laurustinus viburnum. (*V. tinus* 'Eve Price'). This evergreen cultivar produces dark green leaves, white flowers in 3-inch clusters, and dark blue fruits. Plants are 7 feet tall when mature. Zones 7–9.

Onondaga' viburnum (*V. sargentii* 'Onondaga') is deciduous, but hardy as far north as Zone 4. It produces maple-like, bronze-red leaves, white flowers in 5-inch clusters, and bright red fruits that stay on the plant into winter. It has good red fall foliage color. Zones 4–7.

STRIPED SKUNK

The striped skunk is just one of many, many backyard critters that will take advantage of a supply

of berries when they have the chance. While berries make up a relatively small part of the diet of animals like the skunk, they are favorite foods and will be a strong attraction when ripe.

TOUR YOUR NEIGHBORHOOD'S BIRD NESTS

Take a backyard safari with your binoculars so you can identify the many bird nests that have appeared around your property this month.

Style of nest	Outside diameter (inches)	Nest builder
Tiny cup of carefully woven plant fibers, covered with lichens, near the end of a tree branch	1–2 1–1¾	Black-chinned hummingbird, ruby-throated hummingbird
Tiny cup of carefully woven plant down and moss, covered with spiderwebs, on a tree or shrub branch in a thicket	1–2	Anna's hummingbird
Cup of plant down, covered with spiderwebs and lichens, straddling a small tree limb	2–2¾	Blue-gray gnatcatcher
Cup of plant down, lichen and moss, low in a conifer	2–2½	Ruby-crowned kinglet
Cup of plant down, lichen and moss, high in a conifer	2½–2¾	Golden-crowned kinglet
Cup of plant fibers and roots bound together with spiderwebs and lined with hair, in the crook of a shrub	2¾–3	American redstart
Cup of woven fine grasses, lined with hair, in an evergreen shrub, often near a house	4¼–4½	Chipping sparrow
Cup of woven grasses and small plant fibers, lined with thistledown, in the crook of a shrub	2¾–3	American goldfinch
Cup of woven grasses, roots, and bark strips, on the limb of a dense shrub	4½–5¾	Cedar waxwing
Cup of grasses and roots, lined with hair or fine grass, in the crook of a low shrub	5–9	Field sparrow, song sparrow
Cup of grasses, roots and plant fibers, hidden at the base of weeds or grass	3–4	White-crowned sparrow, white-throated sparrow, dickcissel
Cup of grasses, plant fibers and strips of bark, woven onto tall, thick-stemmed marsh plants	4–6	Red-winged blackbird

Style of nest	Outside diameter (inches)	Nest builder
Cup of grasses, roots, plant fibers and hair, hidden under the overhang of a bank or among tree roots	4–6	Dark-eyed junco
Cup of grasses, roots, small sticks and strips of bark in a conifer	3½–5 4–6 4–5	Purple finch, house finch, evening grosbeak
Large cup of woven plant materials, lined with plant down, high up in the crook of a tree	5¼–5¾	Eastern kingbird
Large cup of grasses and plant roots, lined with mud, in the crook of a tree or a flat ledge	6½–7½ 4–5½	Robin, wood thrush
Deep cup of woven plant materials and tree bark, lined with plant down, high up in the crook of a tree	2½–3	Least flycatcher
Cup of woven plant materials, grasses and roots, lined with hair or feathers, in a dense shrub	4–6	Fox sparrow
Collection of grasses, sticks, roots, bark strips and snakeskin or plastic bag strips, in a dense shrub	4–5	Blue grosbeak
Collection of sticks, leaves and other plant materials, lined with mud, fine grasses and fine roots, in the crook of a tree	7–9 6–9	Common grackle, boat-tailed grackle
Loose collection of sticks, in an evergreen or dense shrub	varies widely	Mourning dove
Collection of sticks and vines, usually in the crook of a deciduous tree	7–8	Blue jay
Collection of sticks, vines, grasses and leaves, lined with smaller plant fibers and plant down, in thick shrub or hedge	6¾–8 5–7 5–7 11–13	Mockingbird, northern cardinal, gray catbird, brown thrasher
Large collection of sticks, high up in the crook of a tree	24–27	American crow
Tightly woven, pendant nest of grasses and plant materials attached at rim to deciduous tree branch	4–8 (height)	Northern oriole

mockingbird

robin

dickcissel

MAY

REGION-BY-REGION CHECKLIST

ZONES 2 AND 3 Offer nesting materials like yarn and string to homemaking birds. Seed or reseed your lawn, fertilizing sparingly with compost or organic fertilizer. When your grass reaches 3 inches high, begin mowing with the blade set high. Plant groundcovers, cold-hardy annuals and perennials. Plant trees and shrubs, then mulch around their bases. Prune frost- and winter-killed branches.

ZONE 4 Follow the activity checklist for Zones 2 and 3. Your hummingbird feeder should be getting lots of visitors. Fertilize spring-blooming perennials.

ZONE 5 Follow the activity checklist for Zone 4. Stop feeding suet now. Help feed nestlings by offering soft foods for the parent birds to carry back to the nest, such as fresh-killed mealworms, bits of scrambled egg, small bread crumbs, canned pet food, very finely chopped meats, berries and fruit bits. After spring-blooming shrubs have dropped their blooms, prune them and fertilize with compost. Replace mulch around fruit-bearing trees and bushes.

ZONE 6 Follow the activity checklist for Zone 5. Plant perennials this month. Mulch around bases of trees and shrubs.

ZONE 7 Follow the activity checklist for Zone 6. Plant annuals and fertilize with compost. Plant container-grown perennials. Trim and train vines.

ZONE 8 Follow the activity checklist for Zone 7. Remove early-blooming annuals as soon as flowers drop, unless you want them to set seed and self-sow; replace with late-bloomers like marigolds and zinnias.

ZONES 9 AND 10 Help feed nestlings by offering soft foods for the parent birds to carry back to the nest (See Zone 5). Seed lawn areas. Plant annuals and fertilize with compost. Remove early-blooming annuals as soon as flowers drop, unless you want them to set seed and self-sow; replace with late bloomers. Plant container-grown perennials. After spring-blooming shrubs have dropped their blooms, prune them and fertilize with compost.

CREATE A HUMMINGBIRD GARDEN

When planning a hummingbird garden, there are four things to remember:
red, flower shape, placement, and red.

There's nothing so alluring to hummingbirds as the color red. The tiny birds will examine flowers of other colors and will take nectar from them, but the red flowers will generally draw them first and draw them most strongly. All shades of red, from pink to orange, hold this power, although the most brilliant shades appear to have an edge.

The fragrance of the flowers appears to play only a secondary role in attracting the hummingbirds to feed. Even objects that bear no resemblance to flowers but are shades of red have a strong pull for the birds.

The perfect hummingbird flower

A look at the feeding mechanism of the hummingbird gives us clues about its preferred flower shape and placement. The long needlelike beak and the even longer tongue of the hummingbird have evolved to dip way down into the recesses of deep, tubular flowers to retrieve the nectar. The buzzing, hovering flight pattern of the bird has evolved to allow the hummingbird to feed while in flight. It usually doesn't perch to sip nectar; instead, it opts to hover in place. And this means it prefers not to have to weave its way among stems and leaves to get at the flowers.

Put all of this information together and you have an outline for the perfect hummingbird plant: it produces plenty of reddish, tubular flowers at the outside perimeter of the plant, where the hummingbird can reach them easily.

That's a pretty good description of what many feel is the best overall hummingbird plant: the trumpet vine.

While few of us want an entirely red garden or even an entirely red area of the garden, we can incorporate a great deal of red in our plants. And with just a little planning, we can make use of the different bloom times of various red-flowered plants to greatly extend the hummingbird season in our gardens.

For spring: Lupines, old-fashioned weigela, wild columbine.

For summer: Butterfly weed, coral bells, foxgloves, honeysuckles, Indian paintbrush, mimosa, sweet alyssum.

For summer and fall: Annual phlox, bee balm, butterfly bushes, cardinal flower, common snapdragon, scarlet sage, swamp milkweed, trumpet vine.

Hummingbirds are most attracted to flowers that are red – the redder the better – tubular and growing outward from their stems. The small birds are well adapted to sipping nectar from these flowers.

MAKE YOUR OWN HUMMINGBIRD FEEDER

*Use your knowledge about color and shape when buying or making
hummingbird feeders — simply look for an imitation of the trumpet vine.*

What you'll need

Two large plastic bottles, one with
a base larger than the top
Red acrylic paint
Heavy-gauge wire
Stopper tube (from a hamster or
other small-pet water bottle)
Glue

Here's what to do

1 Take the bottle with a base
larger than the top and paint the
exterior surface with several
coats of red acrylic paint.

2 Turn the bottle upside
down and secure one end of a
length of heavy wire around its
midsection, bending the other
end of the wire up alongside
the bottle and beyond to form
a hanging hook. Insert the
stopper tube into the opening of
the bottle. The feeder should
have a tubular or vaselike
opening where the hummingbird can reach the nectar. And it
should offer open access to that
feeder opening. And, of course,
it should have as much red
surface area as possible.

3 From the second plastic
bottle, cut a six-petaled daisy
shape that's 2 inches in

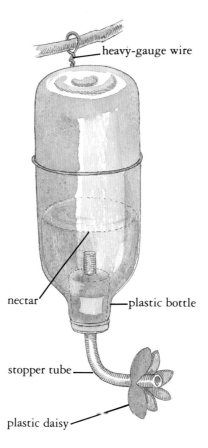

heavy-gauge wire

nectar

plastic bottle

stopper tube

plastic daisy

diameter. In the center of your
plastic daisy, punch a hole
exactly the size of the diameter
of the stopper tube. If the
plastic is not already red, apply
several coats of red acrylic paint.

4 Slide the plastic daisy onto
the tube and bend the petals of
the daisy down toward the end
of the tube. Position the daisy so
the end of the tube extends
½ inch beyond the edge of the

petals and apply glue around
the edge of the hole in the daisy
to hold it in that position.

5 After the glue dries, your
feeder is ready to fill with
hummingbird nectar and hang.
Place your feeders no further
than 15 feet from the nearest
cover and at least 15 feet away
from any window.

6 You can make a nectar
mixture from any type of sugar,
except honey, fruit sweeteners,
or any other common sweetener.
Mix one part sugar to four parts
water. Use non-tap water when
possible, as hummingbirds do
not like heavily chlorinated
water. Never add red dye or food
color to the nectar, or buy a
nectar mix with red dye as this
harms the birds. Bring the
mixture to a boil on the stove,
stirring regularly as you do.
Remove it from the heat as soon
as it begins to boil. After your
nectar cools, it is ready for use.
Store in a refrigerator.

7 Clean the feeder regularly —
every day in hot weather, every
three or four days in cooler
weather. A dental cleansing
tablet in warm water or soap is
best; rinse well afterwards.

HUMMINGBIRDS OF NORTH AMERICA

Allen's
hummingbird

Anna's
hummingbird

Black-chinned
hummingbird

Blue-throated
hummingbird

Broad-billed
hummingbird

Broad-tailed
hummingbird

Buff-bellied
hummingbird

Name	Distribution	Habitat
Allen's hummingbird	Pacific Coast, from Oregon south	Wooded areas
Anna's hummingbird	Pacific Coast, from Canada south and east into Arizona	Wooded and chaparral areas
Black-chinned hummingbird	Western United States, from Canada south	Widespread
Blue-throated hummingbird	Southwestern United States	Wooded areas near water
Broad-billed hummingbird	Western United States	Near wooded areas
Broad-tailed hummingbird	Western United States	Higher elevations
Buff-bellied hummingbird	Gulf Coast of Texas	Along streams
Calliope hummingbird	Western United States	Mountainous regions
Costa's hummingbird	Southwestern United States	Widespread
Lucifer hummingbird	Southwestern United States	Open and desert areas
Magnificent hummingbird	Western United States	Mountain and foothill areas
Ruby-throated hummingbird	East of the Mississippi	Near wooded areas
Rufous hummingbird	Northwestern United States	Wooded areas
Violet-crowned hummingbird	Southwestern United States	Canyons and waterways

Calliope
hummingbird

Costa's
hummingbird

Lucifer
hummingbird

Magnificent
hummingbird

Ruby-throated
hummingbird

Rufous
hummingbird

Violet-crowned
hummingbird

A FIELD GUIDE TO EGGS

It's fun to identify your nesting birds by their eggs. I call it "egg watching."

But only do it at a distance, preferably with binoculars.

Position of nest	Description of egg	Bird
At ground level	White, no markings; elliptical, $\frac{7}{8} \times \frac{5}{8}$ inches	Common ground dove
	White, spotted with reddish brown; oval, $\frac{29}{32} \times \frac{21}{32}$ inches	Rufous-sided towhee
white-throated sparrow	Bluish white, spotted and blotched with brown; oval, $\frac{27}{32} \times \frac{19}{32}$ inches	White-throated sparrow
	Greenish white, spotted and blotched with reddish brown; oval, $\frac{25}{32} \times \frac{19}{32}$ inches	Song sparrow
song sparrow	Tan, heavily spotted, blotched and scrawled with black or brown; pear-shaped, $1\frac{7}{16} \times 1\frac{1}{16}$ inches	Killdeer
In a shrub	Bluish white, spotted and blotched with brown; oval, $\frac{27}{32} \times \frac{19}{32}$ inches	Field sparrow
	Grayish blue, spotted and blotched with brown, gray and purple; oval, $1 \times \frac{23}{32}$ inches	Cardinal
cardinal	Greenish blue, no markings; oval, $\frac{29}{32} \times \frac{11}{16}$ inches	Gray catbird
	Blue-green, spotted and blotched with brown; oval, $\frac{31}{32} \times \frac{17}{32}$ inches	Mockingbird
gray catbird	Blue-green, spotted and blotched with brown; oval, $\frac{3}{4} \times \frac{1}{2}$ inches	House finch
In a tree	White, no markings; elliptical, $\frac{1}{2} \times \frac{11}{32}$ inches	Ruby-throated hummingbird
	White, no markings; oval, $\frac{5}{8} \times \frac{15}{32}$ inches	American goldfinch
northern oriole	Bluish white, scrawled and blotched with brown and black; oval, $\frac{29}{32} \times \frac{19}{32}$ inches	Northern oriole
	Greenish white, scrawled and blotched with brown and purple; oval, $1\frac{1}{8} \times 1\frac{13}{16}$ inches	Common grackle

Position of nest	Description of egg	Bird
In a tree	Blue, no markings; oval, $^{31}/_{32} \times {}^{25}/_{32}$ inches	American robin
	Blue-gray, spotted and blotched with dark brown; oval, $1^5/_{32} \times {}^{27}/_{32}$ inches	European starling
	Olive, spotted with dark brown and gray; oval, $1^1/_8 \times {}^{13}/_{16}$ inches	Blue jay
In a tree, usually a conifer	White, no markings; elliptical, $1^1/_8 \times {}^{27}/_{32}$ inches	Mourning dove
	Bluish green, spotted and blotched with brown, black and purple; oval, $^{11}/_{16} \times {}^1/_2$ inches	Chipping sparrow
In a cavity	White, no markings; oval, $1^1/_{16} \times {}^{13}/_{16}$ inches	Common flicker
	White, no markings; oval, $^3/_4 \times {}^{19}/_{32}$ inches	Downy woodpecker
	White, no markings; elliptical, $^{13}/_{15} \times {}^{23}/_{32}$ inches	Hairy woodpecker
	White, spotted with reddish brown; oval, $^{19}/_{32} \times {}^1/_2$ inches	Black-capped chickadee
	White, spotted with reddish brown; oval, $^3/_4 \times {}^9/_{16}$ inches	White-breasted nuthatch
	White, spotted with reddish brown; oval, $^{21}/_{32} \times {}^1/_2$ inches	House wren
	White, spotted with reddish brown; oval, $^3/_4 \times {}^{19}/_{32}$ inches	Carolina wren
	White, spotted with gray and brown; oval, $^{29}/_{32} \times {}^{19}/_{32}$ inches	House sparrow
	Pale blue, no markings; oval, $^{13}/_{16} \times {}^5/_8$ inches	Eastern bluebird
On a shelflike projection	White, with minimal spots; oval, $^3/_4 \times {}^{19}/_{32}$ inches	Eastern phoebe

American robin

black-capped chickadee

house wren

house sparrow

MAKE A "NATURAL" CONCRETE WATER SOURCE

It's amazing how many choices we have when it comes to providing water in the backyard wildlife habitat, from a simple butterfly puddle or pan of water to this homemade "rock" pool.

Apart from the commercially available birdbaths and pre-formed miniponds, there are many options for making your own water conduits.

You can create wondrous settings around a large boulder, with a natural or carved bowl in its top that you keep filled with water. You can buy your own boulders from many sources, ranging from gardening and landcape centers to vacant lots that are being cleared for construction. They can be had for various prices, sometimes just for the hauling. And they can make attractive centerpieces or special features in a backyard wildlife habitat. On the downside, unless you buy them with transportation included, you'll face the task of moving a few hundred pounds of rock.

If you choose not to buy a boulder, you can always "make" your own. If you start small, you can bring this project off and create a nice little watering pool that will become a virtual wildlife magnet.

What you'll need

1 round flat lid from a 30-gallon plastic trash can
1 round flat lid from a 15-gallon plastic trash can
Chicken-wire fencing
Heavy-gauge wire
Concrete (amount depends on size of structure)
Sheet of plastic

Here's what to do

1 At one edge of the larger lid, use heavy-duty scissors to make a cut from point A to point B to remove that section of the lid.

2 Align one edge of the cut-out area with one edge of the smaller lid, with 1 inch of the cut-out area extending beyond the edge of the smaller lid. Mark lines on the lip of the smaller lid where the edges of the cut-out area from the larger lid touch points C and D. With the scissors, cut along these two lines and then along the bottom edge of the lip of the smaller lid, thus removing that section.

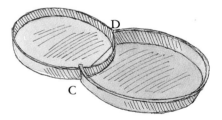

3 Lay the larger lid in the smaller lid, with the extra area of the smaller lid extending under the larger lid. This should give you a two-lid arrangement that resembles a figure 8 with one loop smaller than the other. Use a heavy-duty stapler to attach the two lids where the plastic overlaps and their lips join.

4 With wire cutters, cut sections of the chicken-wire fencing to fit the two lids. Each section of fencing should overlap the other lid by an inch or so. Bend the fencing down in the middle by pushing on it here and there as necessary. Connect the two sections of fencing where they overlap with heavy-gauge wire.

5 Pour the concrete into this mold to the top of the lids at the edges and about half that deep at the centers. Pack it into and through the chicken-wire fencing. Do this quickly before the concrete begins to cure.

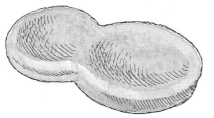

6 After your mold is filled, place it in some out-of-the-way location, cover it with a sheet of plastic and allow it to sit for seven days. Then fill your new pool with water and let it sit for another full day. Pour out the water and scour the concrete with a wire brush to remove any loose bits of concrete from the surface.

7 Turn your mold upside down on the lawn and gently push the concrete structure down and out onto the grass. You're now ready to nestle the artificial rock pool among groundcovers or flowers, into a depression in the lawn or wherever else you want to provide water for your enjoyment and wildlife use.

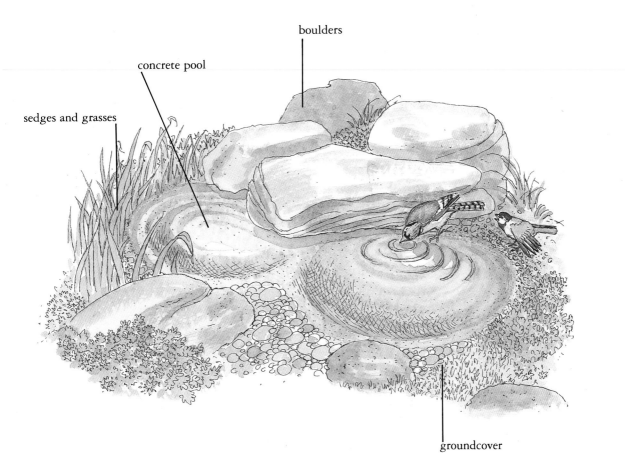

boulders

concrete pool

sedges and grasses

groundcover

BUILD A SIMPLE TOAD SANCTUARY

Toads are great. They're fun to watch, and they patrol our gardens, providing natural pest control as they gobble bugs.

Toads are much maligned. They do not give us warts. They are not slimy. But, when grabbed and threatened, they do release a toxic liquid in self-defense. It's generally only strong enough to irritate the mouths of household pets like dogs and cats, with no lasting damage. It won't irritate your skin – but don't get it in your eyes.

The American toad (*Bufo americanus*) is one of our more cosmopolitan critters, at least in the eastern half of the country. Other common toads are Woodhouse's toad (found in most of the United States); southern toad (found on the southeast Atlantic Coast and Gulf Coast); western toad (found on the Pacific Coast and east into Wyoming and Nevada); and Great Plains toad (found throughout the Great Plains region).

You may already have these toads in your yard. With a couple of notable exceptions, most of these amphibians are widespread across many different habitat types but are generally found in areas that provide cover, moisture and insects. If you can satisfy these three criteria and also provide a biologically sound minipond, where the toads can mate and lay their eggs, your habitat will be irresistible to toads.

Here's how you can build a simple, but effective, toad sanctuary.

What you'll need

Flat rock, at least 8 × 8 inches
6 to 12 fist-sized rocks
Two short sections of terra-cotta
    drainpipe, 3 inches in diameter
3 cups of soft sand

Here's what to do

1 In some sheltered location, preferably near heavy weeds or wildflower cover, dig a hole 8 inches deep and 5 inches in diameter. Then, starting 1 inch above the bottom of the hole and angling up toward the surface of the soil at no more than 30 degrees, dig two 3-inch-wide trenches at opposite sides.

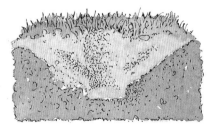

2 Place the drainpipe sections into your trenches, leading all the way from the surface of the soil to 1 inch above the bottom of the hole. Pour the sand into the bottom of the hole.

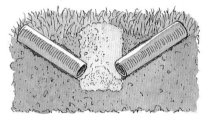

3 Place the flat rock over the top of the hole to form a roof. Use the rest of the rocks to create a rock pile on top of the flat rock, around the surface openings of the drainpipes and between the flat rock and those surface openings.

4 As a variation on this plan, you can add a toad sanctuary beneath any rock wall or rock pile as you're building them, thus eliminating the need to create another rock pile just for this purpose.

5 Toads mostly eat insects, so if you want to attract toads, here's another neat trick: set up a path light, standing 2 or 3 feet off the ground and placed near the edge of a weedy area or flower bed. This will attract the menu items, while allowing the toad to remain under cover until it can snag its prey.

Toads, such as this American toad, are much more common and easy to attract than you might think. They also provide excellent backyard insect control.

JUNE

REGION-BY-REGION CHECKLIST

ZONES 2 AND 3 Offer nesting materials, like yarn and string, and soft foods, like fresh-killed mealworms, bits of scrambled egg, small bread crumbs, canned pet food, very finely chopped meats, berries and fruit bits, for the birds and their nestlings. When danger of frost has passed, plant annuals. Apply compost or another balanced organic fertilizer to annuals and perennials. Rotate critter repellants as necessary around vegetable gardens and ornamental plants that need protection from certain animals. Deadhead perennials and annuals as soon as the flowers fade to maintain a vital supply of nectar for butterflies, hummingbirds and moths. When evergreens like azaleas and rhododendrons have finished blooming, fertilize around their bases with compost. Work existing mulch into the soil and add a fresh layer around trees and shrubs.

ZONE 4 Follow the activity checklist for Zones 2 and 3. Also, prune spring-flowering shrubs after their bloom period is over. Prune any frost-damaged branches on shrubs and trees. Thin fruit on trees. Prune hedges and evergreens.

ZONE 5 Follow the activity checklist for Zone 4.

ZONE 6 Follow the activity checklist for Zone 4. Plant new groundcovers now.

ZONE 7 Follow the activity checklist for Zone 6. Plant next year's perennials now. Mulch perennials for the summer.

ZONE 8 Rotate critter repellants as necessary around vegetable gardens and ornamental plants that need protection from certain animals. Deadhead perennials and annuals as soon as the flowers fade to maintain a vital supply of nectar for butterflies, hummingbirds and moths. Plant new groundcovers now. Fertilize groundcovers with compost. Replace old, faded annuals with new plants, and fertilize the young plants with compost. Deadhead annuals and perennials as flowers fade.

ZONES 9 AND 10 Follow the activity checklist for Zone 8. Prune damaged wood from trees and shrubs. Add mulch around the bases of trees.

CREATE A BUTTERFLY GARDEN

Your flower beds will come alive with butterflies if you plant to provide for your gossamer-winged guests and stop using pesticides and herbicides.

If you really love butterflies, it's easy and fun to create a garden designed specifically to attract and nurture butterflies. The key to success with a butterfly garden is to provide plants for every stage of the butterfly's life cycle. The brightly colored adult butterfly we see fluttering about the garden is just one stage of a process known as metamorphosis. Earlier stages include the egg, caterpillar (the larval stage), and chrysalis (the pupal stage).

Although many species of butterflies do not eat during their adult stage, many others – including a majority of the most common backyard species – do eat in their adult as well as their caterpillar stages. And most species (at least in the caterpillar stage) prefer very specific plants. In the adult stage, the butterfly is generally a nectar drinker. In the caterpillar stage, it eats leaves and occasionally other parts of its host plants.

If you want to develop a fully functioning habitat that will serve all the food needs of your butterfly guests, you should plant and grow a variety of nectar plants for the adults and a variety of food plants for the caterpillars.

Some of the best plants for attracting butterflies include alfalfa, artemisias, asters, black-eyed Susans, butterfly bushes, buttonbushes, coreopsis, daisies, dandelions, dogbanes, goldenrods, iron-weeds, knapweeds, lantanas, mallows, milkweeds (including butterfly weed), mints, passionflowers, privets, purple

The best butterfly gardens provide food plants for caterpillars to munch on and nectar plants for adult butterflies. Many butterflies need different food plants and nectar plants.

coneflowers, Queen Anne's lace, red clover, self-heal, sweet peas, verbenas, vetches and violets. To feed the caterpillars that will become butterflies in your yard, plant apples, artemisias, beans, carrots, dogwoods, hollyhocks, ironweeds, knapweeds, mallows, milkweeds, parsley, passionflowers, pearly everlasting, Queen Anne's lace, sweet peas, vetches, violets and willows. As you can see, some plants attract both butterflies and caterpillars.

Puddling and sunning spots

By providing food and nectar plants, you'll have satisfied the basic needs of the common backyard butterfly species and they will respond. However, there is more you can do to attract butterflies and make them feel at home. Adding puddling and sunning areas are two easy ways to bring butterflies flocking to your yard.

A puddling area is simply a perpetually wet and slightly muddy spot, where the butterflies can alight and take a drink. The spot doesn't need standing water to serve this purpose, since the butterflies will draw what moisture they need from the dampness. There is a growing body of evidence that the mineral content of the moisture — particularly salt — is as important to the butterflies as the moisture itself is. Among the species most likely to take advantage of puddling areas and to congregate there are admirals, anglewings, fritillaries, hackberries, painted ladies, satyrs, skippers and swallowtails.

To the butterfly, the perfect sunning spot is some dry rock or log that's sheltered from the wind but open to the full rays of the sun. The spot should be somewhat protected from would-be predators. A rock or log placed downwind of a flower bed in a place that gets

direct sunlight for several hours each day makes for a prime sunning spot.

A butterfly garden in a container

A butterfly garden can be as large as a meadow or as small as a flowerpot. However, for a container, your plant selection will be more limited than for open ground. Because perennials in containers need winter protection and may dry out or freeze and die anyway, I think annuals, which don't have to be overwintered and can be replanted each year, are a more suitable choice for this project.

In choosing your pot, keep in mind that the darker containers will absorb

Areas of damp soil are attractive to many butterflies. They "drink" both moisture and minerals like salt from the soil.

more heat and dry the soil inside more quickly than lighter-colored it. And, don't forget that whatever pot you choose, you'll have to water it more often than plants in the ground. I check the soil in my containers every day to keep them from drying out. In addition, although you'll want to provide the plants with a fertile soil mix (see "Start Wildflower Seeds Indoors" on page 34) as a starting point, be sparing with additional feedings. That's because your goal with the plants in the butterfly pot is to produce flowers to attract butterflies; a high nitrogen level will cause the plants to put more of their growth into their leaves and stems than into their blossoms.

Sadly, some of the very best butterfly plants have found their way onto our lists of noxious weeds.

BUTTERFLY

To attract as many butterflies as possible, a backyard habitat must provide plenty of nectar plants for the adults and food plants for the caterpillars. Many butterflies have particular preferences. The pipevine swallowtail shown is a fine example – it is named for the plant it eats.

SNAKE! IS IT GOOD OR BAD?

Snakes may not be the best-loved type of wildlife, but most snakes are good for our backyard habitats.

All of our snakes eat a good share of the insects and rodents that many homeowners would like to get rid of. So try not to overreact when a snake is discovered in your backyard.

If you do find a poisonous snake (and of the 115 species native to the United States, only 17 are venomous), call an experienced snake handler from the state wildlife agency to remove it from residential areas and release it unharmed in wilder locales. (Never attempt this yourself!) When children and free-ranging pets are likely to encounter them, even nonpoisonous snakes should probably be removed by an experienced snake handler. Bites from some nonpoisonous snakes can bleed profusely and can become infected, even

though they won't carry any venom. But in an adults-only household, it's usually safe to let nonpoisonous snakes stay in your yard. Most of these snakes won't bite unless you accidentally grab or step on them.

Use a good field guide with photos of the snakes to make a positive identification (at a distance) of any snake that has been found before you decide whether or not to remove it from your yard. See "Recommended Reading" on page 157 for recommended field guides.

General guidelines about the size of the head of a poisonous snake and the like are not definitive enough to rely on. (Though, if you see a rattle, you can be sure it's attached to a rattlesnake!)

Most people would jump back if they saw this small garter snake in their backyard. However, like most snakes that show up in the backyard, it is harmless to humans and will actually help control insects, mice and similar "pests."

BUILD A DRY STREAMBED

Adding a stream of water to your property is quite an undertaking, but a dry streambed takes much less effort and is as attractive to wildlife as it is to you.

A dry stream is a great landscape feature. Smooth rounded rocks and stones are the key to a believable streambed. In a natural stream, running water would grind away all the edges and sharpness over time. Similarly a real stream would naturally follow the contours of your land, moving gradually along the line of least resistance from the highest elevation to the lowest. You don't need to build your streambed across your entire property, but where you do site it, keep this natural flow in mind.

Another natural aspect of most streambeds is their blend of large rocks and small stones. There are almost always many more pebbles and small stones. At the edges of the streams and on the "downstream" side of large rocks, there will usually be sand bars as well. Remember, too, that all streams have banks which slope down to the water. There are, of course, variations along the way, but in general, the slope of a streambed gets deeper toward the middle.

If the course of your imitation streambed happens to bend around and beneath the low-hanging branches of some shrub or small tree, don't avoid the plant. Stay the course and, if it suits the site, take the edge of the streambed right up under the plant. This will add a very natural look to the setting. And, if you're fortunate enough to come to a sharp drop-off, take advantage of that feature as well to create a small "waterfall".

Many critters will take advantage of a dry streambed. Insects, such as butterflies and dragonflies, will sun themselves on the rocks and stones. So will chipmunks. All sorts of insects, amphibians and reptiles, including lizards, will find refuge under and among the rocks.

When adding a dry streambed to your habitat, look to nature for your inspiration. Notice how flowing water has molded this bed.

The collared lizard can be found in most wooded and hilly areas of the American southwest. To attract a collared lizard, provide ample basking

sites with nearby protective cover. This imitates the lizard's natural habitat in rocky ledges and crevices.

CONSTRUCT A SPECIAL SQUIRREL FEEDER

A picnic-table squirrel feeder is fun to watch and will help keep the squirrels busy, diverting at least some of their attention away from your birdfeeders.

It's easy to make your own squirrel feeder. All you need is patience, ¾-inch pine boards and wood screws.

Giving squirrels their own food and feeders will help keep them out of your bird feeders.

What you'll need

One ¾ × 5½ × 26 inch (floor)
One ¾ × 5¾ × 26 inch (back)
One ¾ × 1¼ × 26 inch (front)
Two ¾ × 7 × 16 inch (ends)
Two ¾ × 4 × 4 inch (seats)
Two ¾ × 3 × 3 inch (seat supports)
One ¾ × 4 × 12½ inch (table top)
Four ¾ × 2 × 4½ inch (legs)
Twenty five 1¼ inch wood screws
Two 3½ inch wood screws
Two 3 inch wood screws

Here's what to do

1 Screw the front and back to the floor as shown. The pieces should be flush at the ends and should extend above the floor by 1 inch. Use four 1¼-inch wood screws per joint. Drill ³⁄₃₂-inch pilot holes to make driving the screws easier.

2 Screw the ends to the floor assembly as shown. Use five 1¼-inch wood screws per end.

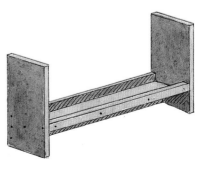

3 Center the seat supports along the front edge of the seats and screw them in place with two 1¾-inch wood screws.

4 Center the seats at either end of the feeder. Screw them in place with two 1¾-inch wood screws driven through each feeder end and one driven up through the floor.

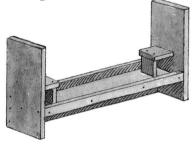

5 Screw the four legs to the corners of the table top, one 1¾-inch screw per leg. Drive two 3½-inch wood screws up through the table top to hold the corn cobs. The screws should be centered from side to side and set in about 2 inches from the ends.

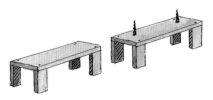

6 Center the table between the chairs and screw it in place with four 1¾-inch wood screws. Drive one screw up through the floor into each leg (see below).

Your squirrels should need no further invitation to eat. Attach the finished table to a feeder pole or tree trunk with a couple of 3-inch wood screws through the rear piece into the supporting structure. Screw a dried cob of corn onto each of the screws extending up through the table top and your two-seater, picnic-table squirrel feeder is ready for use.

JULY

REGION-BY-REGION CHECKLIST

ZONES 2 AND 3 As temperatures climb, wildlife needs water. Set out a pan or saucer of water in a shady spot, or put up a birdbath. Help wildlife find shelter from the sun by setting up a brush pile (see "Set up a temporary brush pile" on page 30), planting shrubs or even turning an old clay pot on its side for little critters. Rotate critter repellents as necessary around vegetable gardens and ornamental plants that need protection from certain animals. Deadhead perennials and annuals as soon as the flowers fade to maintain a vital supply of nectar plants for butterflies, hummingbirds and moths. Make regular tours of neighborhood "wild" sites to observe the plants being used most heavily by butterflies and hummingbirds, and when the flowers fade, begin collecting seeds from those you want to bring into your backyard wildlife habitat. Divide crowded clumps of perennials when the flowers fade. Sow perennials for bloom next summer. Fertilize established trees and shrubs. Take softwood cuttings from shrubs and trees if you want to propagate them.

ZONE 4 Follow the activity checklist for Zones 2 and 3.

ZONES 5 AND 6 Follow the activity checklist for Zones 2 and 3. Plant new grasses and groundcovers. Take cuttings as desired from established groundcovers.

ZONE 7 Follow the activity checklist for Zones 5 and 6. Replace annuals that have finished flowering with other quick-growing annuals that will flower late in the year. Place a summer mulch like compost around the bases of your perennials to help conserve soil moisture. Plant container-grown shrubs and trees. Prune summer-flowering shrubs and vines after their flowers fade.

ZONE 8 Follow the activity checklist for Zone 7. Plant warm-season ornamental grasses like big and little bluestem.

ZONES 9 AND 10 Follow the activity checklist for Zone 8. Cut back spent perennials to encourage new growth and rebloom later this year.

JOIN THE BLUEBIRD TRAIL

What's the most popular nestbox in America? The bluebird box, of course!
Now you can build your own box and become part of the
country-wide network of bluebird trails.

We love to set up bluebird boxes – or even whole trails of boxes – and watch those blue-and-red flashes of color take up residence. We can feel good about our eastern bluebird boxes because they've helped to save this delightful bird from extinction. It was threatened when its natural nest sites – cavities in wooden fenceposts and old trees – were removed to make way for modernization and suburban sprawl. Introduced species like the starling and English sparrow outcompeted the bluebird for the remaining nest cavities. Luckily, the bluebird boxes saved the day – and the bird. Now many state wildlife agencies offer ready-to-assemble nestbox kits at very low prices. And bluebird "trails" of dozens of nestboxes have been set up across the country, on both public and private land.

First, choose a nestbox site
The basic nestbox design, as you'll see from the next project, is very simple. The key to success with bluebird houses is putting them where the birds will actually use them. Bluebirds are primarily insect eaters and need areas of open, short grass, where they can capture the most insects. The area should also provide some scattered, nonobstructive feeding perches, such as isolated trees, fenceposts or power lines. Ideally the nestbox should be within sight of woods.

Place the box on a freestanding pole or post about 4 to 6 feet off the ground,

with its entrance hole facing north or west, away from direct sunlight. If you're putting up more than one bluebird nestbox, space them at least 100 yards apart.

Experience has demonstrated that bluebirds prefer to nest in populations no more dense than that. Additional boxes may actually work to lessen overall use by bluebirds.

Thousands of people across the country have come to the aid of our native bluebirds. Today it's rare to drive on any rural road without seeing at least a few bluebird boxes.

71

BUILD A SIMPLE BLUEBIRD NESTBOX

If you'd like to put up a few nestboxes, it's easy to build your own. Just follow these simple instructions, and you'll soon have the pleasure of seeing bluebirds nesting in your backyard.

What you'll need

¾-inch-thick, rot-resistant board, cut into:

    One 4 × 4-inch floor piece
    Two 4¾ × 10-inch side pieces
    One 5½ × 14-inch back piece
    One 4 × 10-inch front piece
    One 5½ × 8-inch roof piece
Seven 1¼-inch wood screws
¾-inch hardware mesh, cut to
    4 × 10 inches
Two nails

This design allows for easy cleaning. After the bluebirds have fledged their first set of nestlings, immediately clean out the old nest material to encourage them to produce another brood.

Here's what to do

1 Drill ³⁄₁₆-inch (unless stated otherwise) holes in the wood sections, as follows:

Floor:

Drill one hole in each corner for ventilation and drainage and one hole into the center of the ⅜-inch front edge of the bottom.

Sides:

Drill two holes near the top 2 inches from the top and 2 inches in from the side edges for ventilation; drill four holes, one in each corner, 1¼ inches from the top and ⅜ inch in from the edge; drill one hole in the center.

Back:

Drill two holes at the top, 2 inches from the top and 2 inches in from the side edge, and two holes at the bottom, 2 inches from the bottom and 2 inches in from the side edge for attaching the box to the pole;

Front:

Drill one hole at each side, 1½ inches in from the edge and 1 inch down from the top for the nail hinge; two holes into the ¾-inch edges, 1¼ inches from the top; one hole in the center, ⅜ inch from the bottom; and a 1½-inch diameter hole, with its center 2 inches from the top and 2 inches from each side.

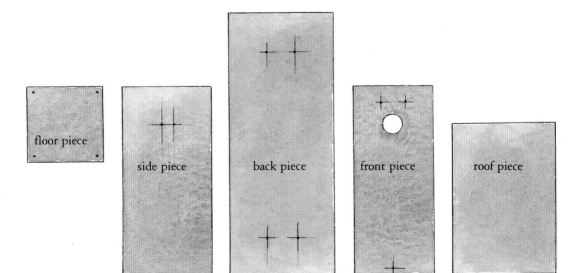

floor piece   side piece   back piece   front piece   roof piece

2 Using two 1¼-inch long wood screws make the following connections: attach the sides to the back, aligning the outer edges of the sides with the edges and top of the back; attach the floor to the sides and back; and attach the roof to the sides and back.

3 Bend the hardware mesh into a box shape, measuring 4 inches by 1 inch, and tack this loosely onto the top of the floor. This will keep blowfly parasites from attacking young nestling bluebirds, as the larvae fall through the mesh and cannot get to the nestlings.

4 Align the holes in the sides with the holes in the edges of the front and slide a nail into each to form a hinge.

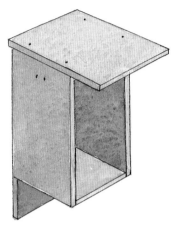

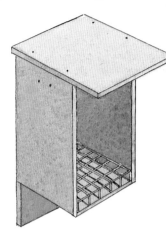

5 Finally, drive a wood screw through the bottom hole of the front into the edge of the floor.

Although much has been written about the perfect bluebird box design, the birds are not nearly as "picky" as was once thought.

PLANNING A MINIPOND

With recent developments in PVC liners, virtually everyone with a backyard, no matter how small it is, can install their own minipond. However, there's much more to a minipond than digging a hole, dropping the liner into place and filling it with water.

Don't be impulsive when you decide to build a water garden. Long before you drive to the local garden center to buy a liner, you should decide on the location and shape of your minipond. Make sure you site it where it's easy to see and enjoy, both from the house and garden. A low-lying spot may seem to be the ideal choice of site. However, unless the area can be built up to a sufficient level, that site could lead to all the runoff from your property and adjacent properties — and whatever chemicals are used on those properties — running directly into your pond. At the other end of the spectrum, you don't want to position the minipond where overflow from the pond runs where it isn't wanted. And remember that a heavily shaded minipond will have trouble producing and maintaining much in the

way of aquatic plant growth, and it will become inundated with leaves every fall.

The shape of your pond must also be considered. The basic circle or square that looks just fine on paper won't have a very natural appearance in the backyard, and a formal or intricate design may lose its detail when installed in the landscape. Irregular shapes with nooks and crannies, minicoves, peninsulas and islands will provide much more attraction for a wide array of wildlife. To help you make your decision, first use rope or garden hose to lay out the planned shape on the actual site. Then make changes as you see fit by repositioning the rope or garden hose. Think as big as your yard permits — a larger pond has more space for plants and wildlife and is no harder to maintain than a 2 × 3-foot water garden.

Supplies for backyard miniponds, from liners and pond shells to a wide variety of plants, have become widely available in recent years. As a result, a minipond, both for wildlife and for beauty, is now well within the reach of most homeowners.

PLANTS FOR A MINIPOND

Common name	Botanical name	Height (inches)	Water depth over crown (inches)	USDA Zones
Anacharis	*Elodea canadensis*	to 36	to 30	5–10
Arrowheads	*Sagittaria spp.*	to 24	to 12	5–10
Blue flag iris	*Iris versicolor*	to 30	to 6	4–9
Bog lily	*Crinum americanum*	to 24	to 6	8–10
Cannas	*Canna spp.*	to 48	to 4	7–10
Carolina fanwort	*Cabomba caroliniana*	to 15	to 24	6–10
Hornwort	*Ceratophyllum demersum*	to 36	to 48	5–10
Lizard's tail	*Saururus cernuus*	to 18	to 6	4–9
Lotus	*Nelumbo spp.*	1–7	2–4	4–10
Marsh marigold	*Caltha palustris*	to 12	to 4	2–5
Pennywort	*Hydrocotyle vulgaris*	to 18	to 12	8–10
Pickerel weed	*Pontederia cordata*	to 30	to 12	3–9
Purple waffle plant	*Hemigraphis colorata*	to 12	to 10	9–10
Red iris	*Iris fulva*	to 24	to 6	5–9
Red ludwegia	*Ludwegia natans*	to 18	to 12	8–10
Ribbon grasses	*Vallisneria spp.*	to 24	to 24	4–10
Scarlet copperleaf	*Alternanthera reinekkii*	to 18	to 12	9–10
Taro	*Colocasia esculenta*	to 40	to 8	8–10
Water arum	*Peltandra virginica*	to 24	to 6	5–9
Water lilies	*Nymphaea spp.*	to surface	to 18	1–10
Water poppy	*Hydrocleys nymphoides*	4–12	4–12	9–10
Water sedge	*Cyperus minima*	to 18	to 6	8–10

arrowhead

marsh marigold

blue flag iris

water lily

MAKING A MINIPOND

The hard work is digging the pond. After that,

you have the pleasure of choosing plants and

then watching the wildlife appear.

Here's what to do

1 The underwater shape of the minipond is just as important as the surface shape, particularly in the backyard wildlife habitat. Steep underwater walls without a ledge, slope or other means of escape will lead many small creatures to drown. If space permits, gradually sloping walls with pebbles and rocks – perhaps even a small log or two angled into the water – will give a much more natural appearance to the minipond, while also adding an element of safety for wildlife. And if you intend for songbirds to be able to drink and bathe at the minipond, it's critical that there are some level, nonslippery surfaces like rocks for them to stand on under no more than ½ inch of water. At its deepest, the pond should be no more than 18 inches to 2 feet, and there should be shallow ledges for plants and rocks.

2 Before you install the liner of your minipond, you want to be certain that the rim of your minipond is level all around.

To do this, place a flat board from one side of the excavation to the other, lay a carpenter's level on the board, and adjust the height of the rim until it's

level, with additional digging as necessary. Then, move the board around a bit, check the level again and adjust. Repeat this until the entire rim has been adjusted. Starting with a level rim will avoid having some of the pool liner jutting out above the water after installation and looking artificial.

3 Install your liner. Manufacturers of PVC liner material provide complete installation details with their products, so I won't cover that aspect of the minipond here.

4 You will need to install a water pump, air pump and filter. If you simply create a pool of water and leave it to its own devices, a stinking, stagnant puddle of watery ooze will result. For a life-filled minipond, the water must circulate. New air needs to be added continuously to keep the water clean. Which pump and filter you choose depends on the size and design of your minipond.

Ask which ones to buy and how to install them at the garden center where you get your liner. (See "Recommended Reading" on page 157 for books on water gardens.)

5 Lining the bottom of your minipond with soil for growing aquatic plants is both dirty and unnecessary. The water in such a minipond will never be completely clear, and filters and pumps will be prone to clogging and breaking-down. You don't need a soil-covered pond bottom to grow aquatic plants. Each plant you want to grow in your minipond can be rooted in a plastic, basketlike container, designed to allow the water to permeate the plant roots and their surrounding soil-mix.

WARNING
Remember that ponds can be dangerous for small children. If you think a small child could gain access to your pond you might want to consider fencing off that area.

6 Plant the container before you put it in the pond. First line the container with a piece of cloth the same way you would line a pie pan with dough. Fill the container, inside the cloth, with heavy soil and position the plant as you fill.

7 Press the growing medium down around the roots and fold the cloth in over the top.

8 Tie the top of the cloth loosely in place around the base of the foliage or cover it with a layer of pea gravel to hold it close over the growing medium.

Tuck cloth around plant and cover it with a layer of pea gravel.

9 Place the plant in its pot in the minipond where desired, but make sure it is at the correct depth. See page 75 for some readily available, easily maintained aquatic plants.

BOX TURTLE

The eastern box turtle is actually found throughout the country as far west as the Great Plains. Box turtles may show up

at any time from spring through fall in just about any backyard within their range. Proximity to a wooded (and often damp) habitat will greatly increase your chances of adding a box turtle to your backyard population.

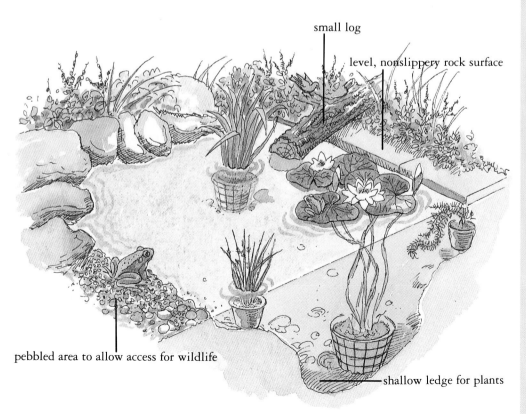

small log

level, nonslippery rock surface

pebbled area to allow access for wildlife

shallow ledge for plants

CHOOSE NATIVE ORNAMENTAL GRASSES

While most tall, seed-producing ornamental grasses will provide shelter, cover and food for various creatures, many commonly available exotic (nonnative) species are highly invasive.

Some of the most popular ornamental grasses have a big drawback: Those huge, showy seedheads can distribute thousands of seedlings, endangering native grasses. (To say nothing of taking over your garden!)

Luckily, many of the native grasses are both beautiful and well suited to backyard gardens. And suppliers have recognized the increasing desire for native American species and are making more of them available each year. Some that you might find at your garden center or in your seed and nursery catalogs are big bluestem (*Andropogon gerardii*), Virginia beardgrass (*Andropogon virginicus*), buffalo grass (*Buchloe dactyloides*), deer grass (*Muhlenbergia rigens*), Indian grass (*Sorghastrum nutans*), little bluestem (*Schizachyrium scoparium*), prairie cord grass (*Spartina pectinata*), prairie dropseed (*Sporobolus heterolepsis*), ribbon grass (*Phalaris arundinacea* var. *picta*), side oats gramma grass (*Bouteloua curtipendula*), switch grass (*Panicum virgatum*) and northern sea oats (*Chasmanthium latifolium*).

Whatever species or cultivars you choose, your wildlife's benefit from these tall ornamental grasses increases directly in proportion to the area given over to these plants. Relatively large expanses of these grasses, possibly mixed with tall wildflowers and shrubs will provide shelter, cover and food for wildlife to a much greater degree than a small patch. The perfect way to use ornamental grasses in the backyard wildlife habitat is to create a wildflower meadow or prairie garden containing a mix of grasses and flowers.

Look closely at any natural wildflower meadow, and you will quickly discover that wildflowers are not the only plants growing there. Usually, most of the plants are tall grasses. Some of these grasses are now available commercially, and nearly anyone can collect seeds from local species in nearby fields.

LIGHT UP YOUR NIGHT WITH FIREFLIES

You can lure more fireflies to your backyard habitat by eliminating all chemicals and allowing some wildflowers and tall grasses to grow in a few areas.

It's easy to see how firefly populations have declined when people of different ages recount their memories of the firefly or lightning bug. You may remember the sparkling light shows put on by masses of these creatures when you were a youngster, while your own children's recollections are generally of much more sparsely lit backyards.

The reliance on pesticides and herbicides for nearly all tasks in the backyard and garden in recent years, and the fashion for very closely cropped lawns have hit the firefly hard. However, there is evidence that the insects are staging a comeback as chemicals are less widely used and new attitudes to informal lawns are adopted. If this trend continues, we can all sit back on July and August evenings and enjoy the show, just like my generation remembers from childhood.

LEARN TO IDENTIFY THE CALLS OF THE WILD

Most of the wildlife attracted to your backyard habitat will bring some sort of voice, sound or call with them.

You can learn to identify different wildlife sounds relatively easily, especially with the many records, cassettes and CDs of wildlife calls now available. Here's a technique I like to try: With an easily focused pair of binoculars in your hands, sit quietly in some spot that gives fairly unrestricted views into most nooks and corners of your backyard wildlife habitat. When you first hear a sound that you want to trace, begin by getting an idea of the general location of the source. Watch that spot and wait for a repeat of the sound. When the critter repeats its call, focus your vision on a more precise spot and bring your binoculars to your eyes.

Scan the area carefully, moving the binoculars ever so slightly as you do.

If you fail to spot the critter on your first try, wait for it to repeat the sound and then repeat the steps above. With this method you can connect the sound to the animal without having to move. This means less chance of creating a disturbance that will send the wildlife scurrying away.

With a little practice and patience you will soon recognize, for example, the chirp of the cricket, the pulsating whistle of the katydid and the courting call of the robin, as well as the startling grunts of the bullfrog and the alarm snort of the doe white-tailed deer.

LIGHT THE GARDEN FOR MOTHS

Beautiful, mysterious moths will bring a whole new nighttime show to your backyard habitat with just a little effort.

From the backyard wildlife perspective, butterflies and moths are welcome visitors to your yard, well worth attracting and nurturing. The pleasure you'll get from watching these lovely creatures will far outweigh their damage.

Many moths are attracted by the same flowers as butterflies, but many more will come to lights. Spotlights and porch lights go a long way toward attracting a wide variety of species. But this concept can be expanded to enhance your garden as well as your backyard moth watching.

In addition to your existing lighting, install a few path lights close to the ground around flower beds and wildflower meadows. These will draw the moths to your feeding sites, provide accents for the garden, and also attract insect-eating amphibians and reptiles. A pole light or two installed around the garden will also attract moths.

Some of the showier moths that might come to backyard lights include the luna moth, cecropia moth, white-lined sphinx, Virginia-creeper sphinx, Pandorus sphinx, imperial moth, io moth and promethea moth. They will be joined by a plethora of smaller species, some of which are very colorful. (See "Recommended Reading" on page 157 for a list of guides to moths.)

Many moths, such as the luna moth (above) and the forester moth (left), are attracted to the backyard habitat by the same nectar sources that lure butterflies to your garden during the day. However, if you add small light sources into your habitat, you'll attract more night-flyers.

DISCOVER THE GARDEN AT NIGHT

When the sun sets and you move indoors for the night, a whole new group of wildlife emerges in your yard.

The nighttime hours offer new possibilities for even the most diverse and mature backyard habitat. Wonderfully scented blossoms with their pale moonlight-reflecting petals are available for an array of nocturnal feeders to take advantage of their nectar. These special night-blooming plants can be grown among the traditional daytime bloomers or, if space permits, in their own moonlight garden.

Some of the most promising possibilities for after-hours flowers are shown below. For maximum moonlight visibility, select cultivars with white, yellow or cream flowers. If night blooms are your goal, it's also important to avoid cultivars of those plants that have been bred specially for daytime opening. If you're designing your own evening garden, put it close to the house where you can enjoy it from indoors. And don't forget garden lighting, a major attraction for night-flyers.

Many "moon flowers," so called because their blooms shine at night, not only attract moths with their scent and appearance but also add a special after-dark feature for human enjoyment.

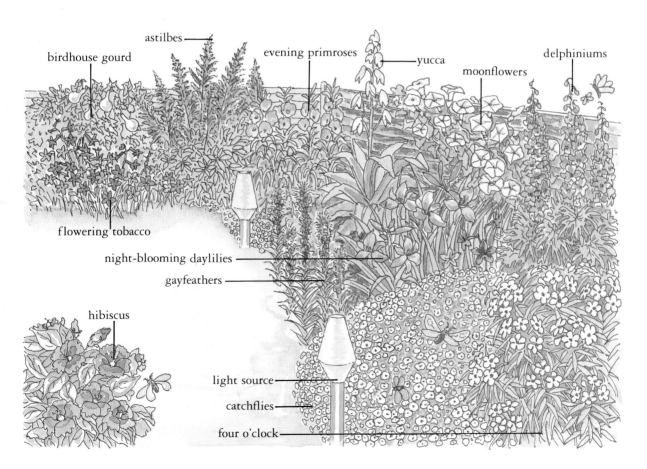

birdhouse gourd
astilbes
evening primroses
yucca
moonflowers
delphiniums
flowering tobacco
night-blooming daylilies
gayfeathers
hibiscus
light source
catchflies
four o'clock

AUGUST

REGION-BY-REGION CHECKLIST

ZONES 2 AND 3 As temperatures climb, wildlife needs water. Set out a pan or saucer of water in a shady spot, or put up a birdbath. Help wildlife find shelter from the sun by setting up a brush pile (see "Set up a temporary brush pile" on page 30), planting shrubs or even turning an old clay pot on its side for little critters. Rotate critter repellents as necessary around vegetable gardens and ornamental plants that need protection from certain animals. Deadhead perennials and annuals as soon as the flowers fade to maintain a vital supply of nectar plants for butterflies, hummingbirds and moths. Make regular tours of neighborhood "wild" sites to observe the plants being used most heavily by butterflies and humming-birds, and when the flowers fade, begin collecting seeds from those you want to bring into your backyard wildlife habitat. Sow new grasses (lawn and ornamental) to give them time to establish themselves before winter. Plant evergreen trees. Take softwood cuttings of shrubs and trees if you want to propagate them.

ZONE 4 Follow the activity checklist for Zones 2 and 3.

ZONES 5 AND 6 Follow the activity checklist for Zones 2 and 3. Plant new grasses and groundcovers. Take cuttings as desired from established groundcovers. Sow perennials now for plants next year. Prune summer-flowering shrubs and vines after their flowers fade. Trim hedges and thickets as needed.

ZONE 7 Follow the activity checklist for Zones 5 and 6. Replace annuals that have finished flowering with other quick-growing annuals that will flower late in the year like flowering kale or nicotiana. Place a summer mulch around perennials to conserve soil moisture. Plant container-grown shrubs and trees.

ZONE 8 Follow the activity checklist for Zone 7. Prune all unwanted suckers and shoots from trees, shrubs and brambles. Mulch around all plants.

ZONES 9 AND 10 Follow the activity checklist for Zone 8. Plant tropical plants now.

WANT TO FEEL LIKE A CHIPMUNK?

Understanding this bright-eyed little critter's habits will help you live in harmony

with its voracious appetite.

What's it like to be a chipmunk? First, picture how much bigger you are than a chipmunk – maybe 100 times its size. Now, visualize taking 100 times 31 kernels of dried, raw field corn and stuffing them into your cheeks. That's the number of kernels that a researcher counted in one chipmunk's cheeks.

Next, imagine spending almost every waking moment of the next couple of days gathering and storing nuts and corn kernels. One observer estimated that he had witnessed the storage of more than a bushel of nuts and corn by a single chipmunk over the course of three days.

The chipmunk is the consummate food-storage machine. Its body is designed to carry considerable quantities of food from whatever source this small member of the squirrel family encounters to its eventual storage site. And the chipmunk's brain seems to contain few thoughts that are not focused on either food gathering and storage or sunning itself on roots and logs. These traits often bring the chipmunk into conflict with gardeners. Many of the bulbs and seeds we plant are seen as nothing more or less than new food sources by the critter. And, since a chipmunk has a relatively small home range (less than an acre in most cases), it will pretty much concentrate its food-gathering efforts on just one or two properties.

As with so many aspects of backyard gardening, encouraging wildlife is a trade-off: are the comical antics of the chipmunk worth the loss of some of our bulbs and seeds? I certainly think so! Don't forget that you can protect bulbs with screening, or plant inedible ones like daffodils. And, of course, the impact of the chipmunk can easily be limited by offering it regular piles of acorns, corn, peanuts and walnuts.

With a little tolerance, you can ignore the chipmunk's bulb-stealing habits and learn to enjoy the comedy and life it adds to your backyard.

GET AN "EDGE" ON WILDLIFE

One of the most important concepts in professional wildlife management circles is the edge effect. The pros discuss it in terms of large natural areas, but it's easy to apply the same idea to your backyard with great success.

What is the edge effect? Put simply, the edge effect occurs when two or more habitat types (like a meadow and woods) come together and their edges merge. Because of that mingling, the edge is usually the area of greatest diversity, in both plant and wildlife species. That means that you'll find more wildlife in an edge area than in either of the two habitats that lead up to it. Plants and creatures that make their living in two or more habitats can meet their basic needs in this new area. In addition, there are those species – both plant and wildlife – that are primarily inhabitants of one type of edge or another.

Because an edge generally marks the area where the denser, more sunlight-starved plants can get their greatest exposure to the sunlight, it is here that some of the most productive plant growth takes place. For example, many forest shrubs that take root in the edge area produce better fruit and foliage than they would in more shaded locales.

Bringing the concept of edge into the backyard can be as simple as no longer mowing a 10-foot-wide strip of grass between your lawn and a hedgerow or thicket. Over several years, that strip will gradually take on some of the characteristics of the hedgerow or thicket, retain some of the characteristics of the lawn and pick up a few new characteristics of its own. A variety of grasses, herbs and wildflowers will grow in your backyard "edge", attracting birds, butterflies, bees and small mammals. Eventually, seedling trees and shrubs will appear. Left to its own devices, over time your edge strip probably would go through the process of succession and become very similar to hedgerow or thicket, as the taller hedgerow plants gradually cast their thwarting shadow over the shorter plants of the lawn.

Keep in mind that an edge has to have a connecting zone between the two meeting habitats to allow the species to mingle. It is not, for example, the area where a lone shrub or tree meets the surrounding lawn, or where the lawn meets a flower bed, or where the garden meets the hedge. With time, the two habitat types could begin to mingle their species and create the edge effect.

Cottontail rabbits are common residents along the edges where grass meets weeds or shrubs. In these areas, they find the mix of food plants, shelter and cover that lets them survive and reproduce. Rabbits are just one of the most obvious species that find everything they need in edges.

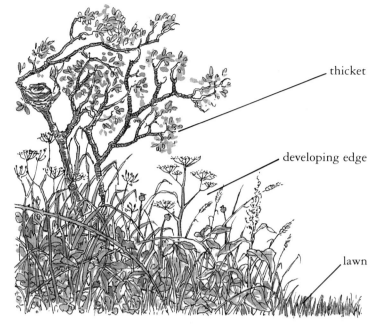

thicket

developing edge

lawn

An area that is slowly reverting from previous human use, such as an abandoned farm, will provide a thorough lesson in the meaning of edge. Growth on such a site will gradually move from (right to left) low grasses and weeds, to taller grasses and weeds, to shrubs to small trees, and eventually to mature forest.

A CRICKET THERMOMETER

It's true! You can get a close idea of the temperature from the chirping of a cricket. But not any cricket will perform this feat, and the exact formulas for pulling off the calculation vary widely.

One species that can be used to tell temperature is the snowy tree cricket, which is widespread across most of the country but which most people would not identify as a cricket on sight.

To do the calculation, count the number of chirps, throbs or pulses the cricket makes in 15 seconds. Add 38 to that number, and you have the approximate temperature in degrees Fahrenheit.

Folklore such as this may not provide an accurate forecast of the weather, but it certainly is an interesting additional footnote in the world of backyard wildlife.

IDENTIFY SPIDERS' WEBS

There are more than 3,000 species of spiders in the United States. You can learn to identify many of them just from their webs. Look closely at the webs in your backyard, then look at the chart below to determine which family each spider belongs to.

Type of web	Spider	Example
Roundish web of concentric, spiraling strands connected to support strands that extend outward from the center	Orb weavers	Garden spider
Flat, sheetlike web	Sheet-web weavers	Hammock spider
Flat, sheetlike web with a funnel reaching from the center to one side	Funnel-web weavers	Grass spider
Irregular web with strands of silk over captured prey	Comb-footed spiders	Black widow spider
Irregular web among leaves, in small openings or on plant stems	Dictynid spiders	Branch-tip spider
Irregular web under tree bark or under stones	Violin spiders	Brown recluse spider
Baglike, tube-shaped web under stones or in the curl of a leaf	Sac spiders	Ant mimic spiders
No web	Crab spiders, jumping spiders, lynx spiders, trap-door spiders, wandering spiders, wolf spiders	

KEEP SOME AREAS OFF-LIMITS

Do your backyard bird guests insist on going where they are not wanted, like your vegetable garden or around your blueberries or cherries? Bird netting isn't the only answer. You can scare birds away from off-limits areas with a predator "decoy."

Keep birds away from off-limits areas by setting out predator decoys – plastic owls or inflatable snakes. The trick to using these decoys successfully is to change not only their position within the backyard and garden but also their body angle.

If you make these changes every day during harvest season, you'll prevent the birds from quickly becoming accustomed to the decoys and unafraid of them.

Selected areas of the backyard, like the vegetable garden, can be placed off-limits to wildlife through fencing, scare devices, and repellents. For birds, a slithering snake "decoy" can be a strong repellent.

PLANT A BIRDSEED GARDEN

If spilled seeds sprout vigorously around your feeder, try this easy plan for putting the weedy tendency of the various seeds in bird feeding mixtures to work for you and your backyard birds.

One of the problems with backyard birdfeeding is the myriad small plants that spring up all around the feeding area. Heavy growth can develop each summer to the detriment of your grass and garden. However, when you plant and tend them like garden seeds, the sunflower, safflower, millet, milo and corn in birdseed will produce lush growth and an ample seed supply for the fall and winter. You can plant your birdseed garden in neat rows or in wild-looking patches or corners. Prepare the soil just as you would for the wildflower meadow. (See "Develop a small-scale wildflower meadow" on page 44.)

You can start with packets of individual seeds or separate the different seed types from a general mix by hand. Most types of birdseed develop into large plants, so give them plenty of room to grow. Leave at least a foot between rows; within the rows, sow sunflower seeds at least a foot apart and corn, millet, milo and safflower at least 6 inches apart. Because of their respective heights, you will want to arrange them as follows in relation to the direction of the sun's rays: tall-growing sunflower in the most northerly position at the back, then corn, then milo, then millet and finally lower-growing safflower in the most southerly position at the front. Also, to ensure wind pollination that will produce the ears, plant a block of five short corn rows rather than just one.

As these seeds are intended for eating, not planting, you have no guarantees about the germination rates. To increase the odds in your favor, drop three or four seeds into each of your planting holes. If

A birdseed garden, planted like a traditional backyard vegetable garden, will have a traditional look while providing an enormous amount of food for a wide variety of birds. You can leave the seedheads in place or harvest them for use in your feeders; the birds will appreciate either method.

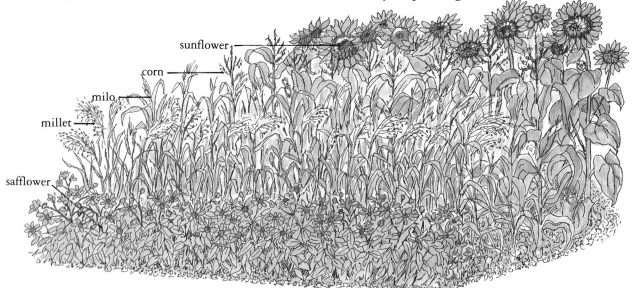

sunflower

corn

milo

millet

safflower

The northern cardinal
is one of our most
welcome backyard
visitors. The best way
to attract the bright
red bird and his

*Sunflowers are favorite sources of food for birds
and other critters. They're easy to grow, too.*

all the seeds in a hole sprout, use small scissors to trim off all seedlings but one soon after they come up.

Harvest your birdseed

At harvest time you face a basic decision – what to do with the seed. You can just leave the seedheads and ears on the plants for the birds to pick at over the next few months. (If you choose this option, careful placement of the growing site is essential as this may look unsightly.) You can also harvest full seedheads and ears, store them and put them out throughout the birdfeeding season. A third option is to harvest the seedheads and ears and then strip off their seeds or kernels.

Regardless of the form in which they are harvested, the seedheads and ears or seeds and kernels must be properly dried to prevent molds or mildew from developing in storage. Hang the seedheads or ears in a sheltered, but well-ventilated location, such as under the roof of a porch or patio. Spread individual seeds or kernels on trays in a warm, dry place and make sure you shift and turn the seeds or kernels every few days until they are thoroughly dry.

Store the seedheads, ears, seed or kernels in a dry, mouseproof place until birdfeeding time comes round again. Large metal canisters are great for birdseed storage and are often available from bird and pet supply stores.

browner mate, is by
hanging a small
feeder stocked with
safflower seeds within
easy flying distance of
evergreen shrubs or
trees.

SEPTEMBER

REGION-BY-REGION CHECKLIST

ZONES 2 AND 3 If you haven't already done so, fertilize established lawn areas and ornamental grasses with a topdressing of compost. Plant new groundcovers and fertilize with compost. Continue to deadhead those annuals and perennials that are still growing to encourage rebloom. Pull up spent plants from annual flower beds and border areas. Plant new perennials. Unless perennials have decorative seedheads, cut them back when they have finished flowering. Prepare areas and plant bulbs now. Clean up debris from your more formal garden areas but leave it in place to provide cover for wildlife in more out-of-the-way spots. Clear and till the vegetable garden so it's ready for next year. Water new shrubs and trees, as needed, to encourage good root growth before the onset of winter. It's not too early to set out birdfeeders, but wait until next month to start feeding suet.

ZONE 4 Follow the activity checklist for Zones 2 and 3.

ZONE 5 Follow the activity checklist for Zones 2 and 3. Plant new perennials and water all new plantings regularly. Divide crowded perennials and replant divisions.

ZONE 6 Follow the activity checklist for Zone 5.

ZONE 7 Follow the activity checklist for Zone 5. Plant new trees and shrubs.

ZONE 8 Follow the activity checklist for Zone 7.

ZONES 9 AND 10 Plant cool-season grasses. Plant new perennials and water all new plantings regularly. Fertilize late-blooming perennials with a topdressing of compost. Divide crowded perennials and replant divisions. Plant new trees and shrubs. Trim hedges and thickets as needed. Prune out damaged branches from trees and shrubs. Use the prunings to make brush piles, so wildlife will have a place to shelter over winter. Take cuttings from evergreen trees and shrubs if you want to propagate them.

CHOOSE THE BEST PLANTS FOR FALL COLOR

Just because you're choosing plants to benefit wildlife doesn't mean you can't have a beautiful landscape. Here are some of the best plants for both wildlife and brilliant fall color.

Red leaves:
Black chokeberry (*Aronia melanocarpa*)
Tupelo, sour gum (*Nyssa sylvatica*)
Burning bush (*Euonymus alata*)
Heucheras (*Heuchera* spp.)
Crape myrtle (*Lagerstroemia indica*)
Downy serviceberry (*Amelanchier arborea*)
Flowering dogwood (*Cornus florida*)
Highbush blueberry (*Vaccinium corymbosum*)
Little bluestem (*Schizachyrium scoparium*)
European mountain ash (*Sorbus aucuparia*)
Red-osier dogwood (*Cornus sericea*)
Switch grass (*Panicum virgatum*)
Scarlet oak (*Quercus coccinea*)
Sumacs (*Rhus* spp.)
Sweet azalea (*Rhododendron arborescens*)
Sweet gum (*Liquidambar styraciflua*)
Deciduous viburnums (*Viburnum* spp.)
Virginia creeper (*Parthenocissus quinquefolia*)

Orange leaves:
Barberries (*Berberis* spp.)
Red chokeberry (*Aronia arbutifolia*)
Sugar maple (*Acer saccharum*)
Yellow or gold leaves:
Birches (*Betula* spp.)
American bittersweet (*Celastrus scandens*)
Cherries (*Prunus* spp.)
Columbines (*Aquilegia* spp.)
Ginkgo (*Ginkgo biloba*)
Hostas (*Hosta* spp.)
Northern sea oats (*Chasmanthium latifolium*)
Redbuds (*Cercis* spp.)
Summersweet (*Clethra alnifolia*)
Switch grass (*Panicum virgatum*)
Tulip tree (*Liriodendron tulipifera*)
Winterberry (*Ilex verticillata*)
Wisterias (*Wisteria* spp.)
Witch hazels (*Hamamelis* spp.)

An important consideration in choosing shrubs and trees for your backyard — in addition to their value in providing food, cover and shelter for wildlife — should be their fall leaf color. Brilliantly colored autumn foliage can light up your landscape as much as flowers.

T AKE A CLOSE-UP LOOK AT WILDLIFE

Those wonderful, tack-sharp, close-up photos of wildlife you admire so much in your favorite nature magazines look so good because of a few professional secrets that you might find useful.

Here are some professional tricks that you can use to take great photos in your own backyard: Many of those animals are photographed while at food baits. Many are photographed by a photographer hidden in a blind. Most are photographed with long telephoto lenses. And most good shots require a great deal of time and patience on the part of the photographer.

In your backyard habitat, you're already providing the bait, either in the plants you grow or the food you offer. You're already observing the animals on a daily basis and can predict their timetable and actions with reasonable accuracy. You may not have a long telephoto lens (300mm minimum), since they are expensive. You may not even have a 35mm, single-lens-reflex camera that will function with that lens. However with most of the wildlife that comes to your backyard, you can overcome the lens handicap to some extent and produce quite acceptable photos with the point-and-shoot camera you probably already have on hand. The key to success with a point-and-shoot camera is the blind.

Make your own blind

While there are many photo or hunting blind designs available commercially, with price tags ranging from $30 to $40 all the way up into the hundreds of dollars, making your own is both cheap and easy.

Many professional-quality photography blinds are available in a wide price range.

What you'll need

43 feet of camouflage-printed
    fabric, cut into:
    Two 16½-foot lengths
    Two 5-foot lengths
4 wooden poles, 6 feet long ×
    1 inch (or more) in diameter
Thumbtacks
Large safety pins

Here's what to do

Choose a spot a few feet from the feeder or area of your habitat most regularly visited by the wildlife you want to observe or photograph close up.

1 Drive your four poles into the ground, 4 feet apart to form a square. Drive the poles about a foot into the ground, leaving about 5 feet above ground.

2 Attach one end of one 16½-foot length of fabric to one of the poles with thumbtacks so that the bottom of the fabric touches the ground. Then stretch the fabric around all of the poles to form the sides of a square, with the loose end of the fabric overlapping the starting point.

Connect the fabric to each of the poles with a few thumbtacks. Attach the loose end overlap with a couple of large safety pins.

3 Repeat this process with the second 16½-foot length, placing it above the first, but with some overlap. Use a few safety pins to connect this to the lower piece here and there to prevent any gaps from developing.

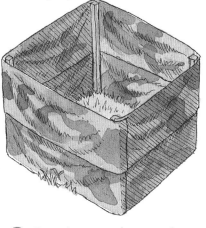

4 Lay the two shorter pieces of fabric over the top of the fabric walls to create a roof for your blind. Use safety pins to connect the two shorter pieces to one another and to the walls at several places.

5 Using the area of the overlapping fabric as your door, disconnect the safety pins, enter the blind and reconnect the door with the pins.

6 With scissors cut several small rectangular flaps in the fabric that faces the area you want to watch. The flaps need to be level with your eyes when you sit on a chair. These are your viewing portals. The fabric can be taped or pinned up out of the way when you're using the blind or allowed to drape down over the barrel of a camera lens poking through the opening.

7 Let the blind sit unoccupied for several days until the animal you want to get close to resumes its normal activities. Then, in advance of the critter's expected arrival time, make yourself comfortable in the blind and get ready for some special moments.

KEEP YOUR PATHWAYS NATURAL

Well-placed paths will make it easy and enjoyable for you, your family and friends to stroll through your backyard habitat. Paths bring you closer to the wildlife in your landscape.

Paths encourage you to walk around instead of just watching from the deck or porch. A path can also make it a lot easier to reach hard-to-maintain areas like clumps of shrubs or boggy sites. Another great thing about them is that they can make your backyard habitat more exciting: As you follow the trail through your woods or wildflower meadow, you never know what surprises are waiting around the bend.

A trail with a natural look will blend best with most other backyard habitat elements. So before you begin, take a nature walk and study some trails and paths in the wild. Note that they don't have manicured edges – plants spill over onto the trail. They aren't edged with stones. And they generally are made of a variety of materials. Borrow whatever ideas you like from the wild trails.

Before choosing a path material, consider the backyard habitat through which the pathway will wind. In nature, the materials that make up the surface of trails usually have been supplied by the natural elements immediately around the trail. For example, a trail through a pine forest usually is covered with pine needles, while one through a deciduous forest would be covered with leaves and moss. A dry creek bed would be covered with smooth rocks and pebbles. Matching the path surface to its surroundings will give your trail a much more natural feel.

Actually, you have a wide variety of surface materials from which to choose. The most permanent and lowest-maintenance choice is concrete, which

Whether covered with wood chips, mulch, grass or bare soil, a pathway through a wildlife habitat area will have a more comfortable feel if it is designed, built and maintained to look natural. The pathway will "feel" like it belongs there and will actually enhance the wildness of the overall setting.

AMERICAN
GOLDFINCH

The American
goldfinch is a big
endorsement for
feeding backyard
birds year-round.

During the winter,
the male is a dull
greenish brown. But,
spring through
summer, that same
male takes on the
bright lemon-yellow
color for which the
species is named.

can be given a natural appearance by imbedding local stones in its surface. Grass can be almost as permanent as concrete for paths that don't get a lot of foot traffic. Wood chips have a very natural look as a trail surface, but you'll need to add new chips regularly as the old ones break down. (Of course, you can always remove these "composted" old chips and use them as mulch!) Over relatively flat surfaces, log or board pathways can be attractive, natural-looking and long-lasting. In general, bare soil is the poorest choice, since it's impossible to pack soil down hard enough so that rains won't wash it out and create potholes.

Regardless of the surface material or materials you choose to put down, always give your pathway a crown. This means that the surface material should be laid so that the center of the trail is raised slightly higher than the sides. The raised center, or crown, will allow water to run off into the landscape, preventing puddles and gullies from forming on the trail, and washing out your path material.

If your pathway winds behind some thick habitat element, such as a planting of shrubs, trees and vines, you have the perfect place to create a hidden alcove away from the rest of the world. Such a secluded position is ideal for a bench, where you can sit peacefully and listen to the songbirds all around you. If size permits, your secluded spot could also be the perfect location for one of the many wildlife feeders described in this book. See pages 21 and 25 for examples.

CLEAN UP WITH WILDLIFE IN MIND

Leaves, and dead, broken twigs and branches are scattered everywhere. One Saturday morning, we erupt from bed and declare, "It's time to clean up the yard!"

This year, resist the urge to rake everything clean, cut down all your perennials and ornamental grasses, and dump all those debris-filled trash bags on the curb for pickup. Clean up your yard with the critters' needs in mind.

Leave seedhead-forming perennials like coneflowers and black-eyed Susans in place over winter. Leave your ornamental grasses standing, too. As winter comes on, you'll be surprised by how much you appreciate the winter interest these plants provide in the landscape. And birds and other wildlife will appreciate the seeds.

Don't cut down your wildflower meadow until spring. That little field of flowers and grasses is a great winter wildlife habitat.

Don't bag those leaves! Shred them for composting or weed-smothering, water-conserving mulch. Shredded leaves make a great mulch for backyard habitat gardens because they look so natural.

Leave some of the leaves under the hedge at the back corner of the property in place. They'll provide homes for overwintering insects, which in turn will provide a source of food for many birds, mammals and other insect-eating critters.

Make fallen twigs and limbs into a small brush pile in some out-of-the-way spot, where the neighbors won't view it as an eyesore. A brush pile will quickly attract a surprising variety of wildlife. (For more on brush piles, see page 30.)

Many critters, like this ground skink, come quickly to areas where leaf litter has been left on the ground. Leaf litter is part of their normal habitat. Backyards that are completely cleared from one fence to the other are much closer to wastelands than they are to wildlife habitats.

CHOOSE THE RIGHT BINOCULARS

When you buy binoculars, choose a pair that will let you enjoy watching small insects as well as birds and mammals, and one with as much light-gathering ability as possible.

Binoculars are a great tool for watching your wildlife visitors from a distance. The key is choosing a good pair. You can find both the magnification and the light-gathering specifications in a set of numbers printed on every pair of binoculars. The power of the binoculars, expressed as the number before the letter ✕, is the magnification factor. This number tells you the number of times the binoculars will magnify what you look at through the lenses. In other words, a pair of 7✕ binoculars will magnify images seven times. A power of 7✕ or 8✕ should be strong enough to meet all your backyard needs.

The number after the ✕ tells you the size of the lens in the binoculars. Usually 30 or 35, this number is a measurement in millimeters. But all you really need to know is that the larger this number is, the better the light-gathering ability of the binoculars. And the more light your binoculars let in, the better you'll be able to see wildlife and other images viewed under low-light conditions.

A third number that is found printed on binoculars near the magnification and light-gathering numbers represents the field of view for the image seen through the binoculars. It can be shown as degrees or as width in feet when something is viewed from 1,000 yards away. The larger the figure, the wider the field of view. Wide fields of view permit easier and quicker spotting of the target, while narrower fields eliminate extraneous details but make focusing more difficult.

When choosing binoculars, don't forget weight. The more a pair weighs, the harder it is to hold steady. Make sure the pair you choose is comfortable when you hold it for several minutes, or you'll get the "shakes" and lose your bird or other quick-moving critter.

Lens coating is the final critical factor for you to bear in mind. Hold the binoculars under fluorescent light and look at the lens opening, which is opposite the eyepiece. It should look purple or amber. If it looks white, it is not coated properly.

Even in the tiniest backyard wildlife habitat, such as on an apartment balcony, binoculars can add a great deal to your enjoyment of wildlife. With the magnification of binoculars, you'll see many small details that the naked eye would certainly miss.

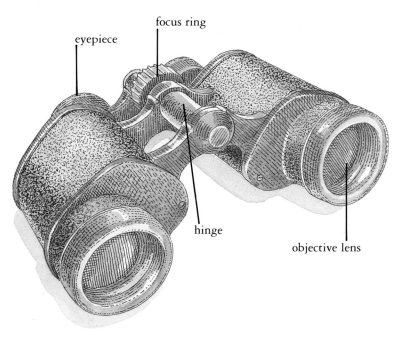

eyepiece

focus ring

hinge

objective lens

OCTOBER

REGION-BY-REGION CHECKLIST

ZONES 2 AND 3 Set out birdfeeders if you haven't already. Fill suet feeders. Continue watering new groundcovers and grasses as needed, but stop as soon as ground shows signs of freezing. Deadhead perennials and annuals as soon as flowers fade. Cover perennial beds with winter mulch and mulch around shrubs and trees. Stake newly planted shrubs and trees to support them in winter gales. Add tree guards to young shrubs and trees to prevent their bark from being damaged by wildlife. Enjoy this year's spectacular fall foliage show.

ZONE 4 Follow the activity checklist for Zones 2 and 3. After trees have lost their leaves, take hardwood cuttings from shrubs and trees if you want to propagate them.

ZONE 5 Follow the activity checklist for Zone 4.

ZONE 6 Continue watering new groundcovers and grasses as needed. Deadhead perennials and annuals as soon as flowers fade and stop watering as the plants go dormant. Plant new shrubs and trees, watering as needed. The autumn hawk migration is in full swing this month – don't miss it!

ZONE 7 Plant new groundcovers and grasses, watering as needed. Apply compost or another balanced organic fertilizer to existing groundcovers and grasses. Plant new perennials. Divide clumps of established perennials that have become crowded and replant divisions. Deadhead perennials and annuals as flowers fade. After trees have lost their leaves, take hardwood cuttings from shrubs and trees, if you want to propagate them.

ZONE 8 Follow the activity checklist for Zone 7. Plant or transplant hardy annuals. Plant new trees, shrubs and vines, watering as needed.

ZONES 9 AND 10 Follow the activity checklist for Zone 8.

PREDICT WINTER TEMPERATURES

According to folklore, the woolly bear caterpillar — the larval stage of the Isabella tiger moth — can forecast the coming winter temperatures.

Supposedly, the wider the black bands on the woolly bear caterpillar, the colder the winter. Find an all-black woolly bear, and you'd better put in plenty of extra firewood! But, despite evidence compiled by long-time observers of the woolly bear, the amount of black on the caterpillar is probably more a function of current conditions than of weather to come. Younger caterpillars generally have wider black bands than more mature specimens. Early cold temperatures probably urge a larger number of youngsters to crawl around in search of their winter quarters and, incidentally, bring them into the sight of human beings.

Folklore tells us that the wider the black bands on the woolly bear caterpillar, the colder our winter will be.

DON'T WASTE YOUR JACK-O-LANTERN

As you carve your Halloween pumpkin this year, don't overlook the treasure trove of goodies for wildlife that you find among the pulp you remove.

Pumpkin seeds are a delight for the many bird species that relish large seeds, including jays, nuthatches and grosbeaks. Simply separate the seeds from the pulp, then wash them under the kitchen faucet. Dry them on a cookie sheet in the oven or spread them in the sun. Offer the pumpkin seeds to the birds immediately, or store them as you would any other birdseed, keeping them dry.

The shell of the pumpkin also makes a very welcome wildlife treat after Halloween. If you have some secluded spot in the backyard where the decaying pumpkin won't be too much of an eyesore, place it on the ground and watch it disappear bite by bite. For a tidier setup, cut the pumpkin into small squares and offer them on the ground and in your feeders.

BUILDING A BAT BOX

If mosquitoes, gnats and other flying insects are a problem, few natural controls are more effective than bats. The best way to build a local population is by making these winged wonders a bat box.

What you'll need

¾-inch lumber cut into:

Two 10¼ × 27-inch side pieces

One 20 × 23-inch front piece

Three 18¾ × 20-inch roosting boards

One 20 × 27-inch back piece

One 20 × 7¼-inch inner roof

One 22½ × 10¾-inch roof piece

Bark, cut into 22 × 18½-inch strips

¾-inch wood screws

Forty-two 1½-inch wood screws

Note: There is no floor in a bat house, since the bats enter from beneath.

Here's what to do

1 Cut the top of each side at an angle so that a slanted top results (4 inches or less at the front).

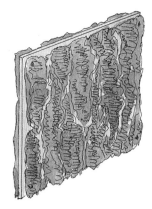

2 Drill six ¼-inch diameter holes through the front, spacing them evenly in a line 3 inches from the bottom.

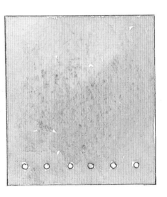

3 Attach the strips of bark to both sides of each roosting board, covering as much of the surfaces as possible. Connect each bark strip to the boards with two ¾-inch wood screws.

4 Attach one side to the back, using four 1½-inch wood screws. Repeat with the second side.

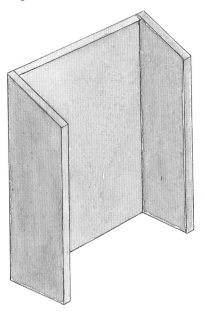

5 Position one roosting board 1⅜ inches in from the back and ¾ inch down the sides. Attach it with three 1½-inch wood screws through each side into the roosting board.

6 Position the second roosting board 1⅜ inches in front of the one you have installed, and attach it in the same way.

7 Position the third roosting board 1⅜ inches in front of the second board and attach it in the same way.

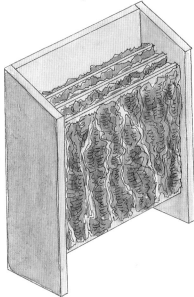

8 Attach the front to the side pieces with four 1½-inch wood screws through the front into each of the sides. Position the inner roof on the roosting boards and screw in place.

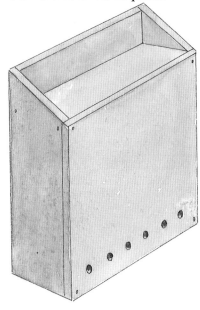

9 Connect the outer roof to the front, back and side pieces with two 1½-inch wood screws through each piece.

10 Using standard fixings, position the bat box on a tree, the side of your house or a sturdy pole, at least 20 feet above the ground.

BROWN BAT

Like other bats, the little brown bat eats a huge number of flying insects every night. It

can catch and eat 600 mosquitoes in just one hour! The little brown bat locates its prey and avoids obstacles by emitting high-pitched radarlike sounds that bounce off objects in its path.

COMMON BATS IN THE UNITED STATES

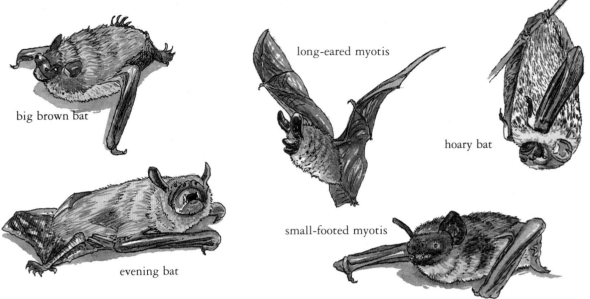

big brown bat

long-eared myotis

hoary bat

evening bat

small-footed myotis

Common name	Scientific name	Region
Big brown bat	*Eptesicu fuscus*	Nearly all of the United States
Eastern pipistrelle	*Pipistrellus subflavus*	Eastern half of the United States
Evening bat	*Nycticeius humeralis*	Eastern half of the United States except New England
Hoary bat	*Lasiurus cinerus*	All of the United States except southernmost Florida
Indiana myotis	*Myotis sodalis*	New England, south and west through the Midwest
Little brown bat	*Myotis lucifugus*	Most of the United States except Florida, Texas and southern California
Long-eared myotis	*Myotis evotis*	All of the United States west of the Rocky Mountains except southern California and New Mexico
Long-legged myotis	*Myotis volanus*	Western half of the United States
Red bat	*Lasiurus borealis*	East of the Rocky Mountains and in the Southwest
Small-footed myotis	*Myotis leibii*	New England, Appalachian Mountains and the western United States

SEE THE WONDERS OF MIGRATION

Many Americans live within an easy drive of some spot where, in a single day, they can watch hundreds of hawks, eagles and falcons riding the air currents in fall and spring.

Birds of prey are spectacular. It's fun to see how many of these majestic birds you can recognize from their silhouettes alone – and with binoculars, you can often see more detail, even though many birds of prey fly amazingly high up. (It's not unusual for airplane pilots to see passing eagles and falcons!)

Among the best known and most frequently visited hawk-watching sites in the United States are Hawk Mountain, Pennsylvania; Cape May, New Jersey; and Hanging Rock Migratory Raptor Observatory, West Virginia. However, there may be a less-well-known hawk-watching site much closer to your home. You'll find one of these sites more easily if you keep in mind that the birds are taking advantage of natural features which cause a strong updraft in the wind. In the East this means the mountain ridges and the coastline, particularly when a passing cold front moves through from the Northwest. The broken mountain ranges of the West are less conducive to hawk, eagle and falcon migration, but many prominent ridges do see their share of passing birds, particularly when a strong southwest wind blows.

While hawks, such as this red-tailed hawk, are not regular visitors to most backyard habitats, watching their annual migrations can be enjoyable for any nature enthusiast. Suitable viewing sites probably are within a reasonable drive from your home.

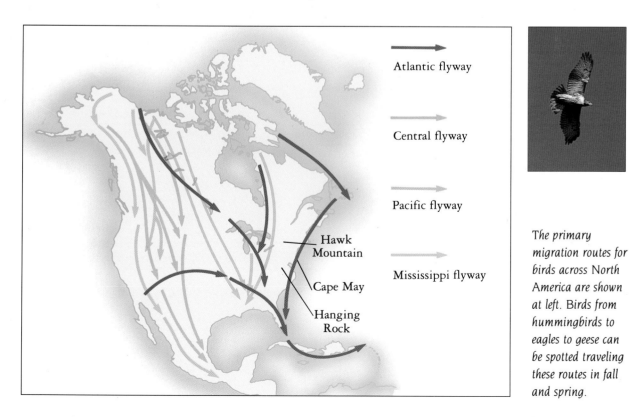

Atlantic flyway

Central flyway

Pacific flyway

Mississippi flyway

Hawk Mountain

Cape May

Hanging Rock

The primary migration routes for birds across North America are shown at left. Birds from hummingbirds to eagles to geese can be spotted traveling these routes in fall and spring.

BUILD A BUTTERFLY HIBERNATION BOX

Encourage adult butterflies to hibernate or seek shelter in your backyard wildlife habitat by providing them with this easy-to-make butterfly hibernation box.

All regions of the United States have some butterfly species that will hibernate locally through the winter in their adult stage. Some of the more common butterflies that hibernate in the United States are the mourning cloak, question mark and comma butterflies. In addition, many more species will take shelter during periods of sudden coolness from spring through fall.

What you'll need

¾-inch lumber, cut into:
    Two 8½ x 24-inch side pieces
    One 7 x 23-inch front piece
    One 7 x 24-inch back piece
    One 7 x 7-inch floor piece
One 3 x 23-inch center post
One 10 x 11-inch roof piece
Twenty 1½-inch wood screws
One 2-inch wood screw
Bark, cut into strips
¾-inch wood screws

Here's what to do

1 Cut the top of each side at an angle so that a slanted top results. Cut a slit 2 inches long × ⅜-inch wide toward the bottom of each side.

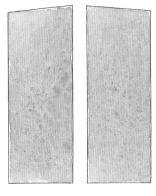

2 Cut six 1½- × ½-inch-wide slits through the front.

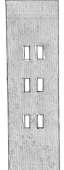

3 Cover as much as possible of the side pieces and back of the box, and both sides of the center post with bark strips. Drive two ¾-inch wood screws through each bark strip into the wood. Trim the bark strips with a sharp knife so they fit tightly against the wood surfaces. Leave the openings in front of and behind the center post.

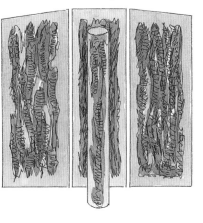

4 Align the two sides and the back with the bottom of the floor and attach each to the floor with two 1½-inch wood screws.

⑤ Attach the center post to the center of the floor with one 1½-inch wood screw driven through the floor into the bottom of the post.

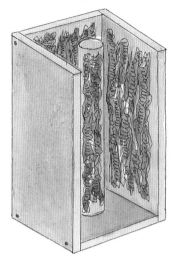

⑥ Leaving a 1-inch overhang on all sides, attach the roof to the sides and back using two 1½-inch wood screws for each piece. Attach the roof to the center post with one 2-inch wood screw. (Don't worry about the slight gap left between the roof and the center post.)

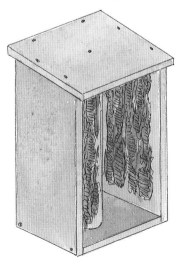

⑦ Attach the front to the sides, floor and roof with two 1½-inch screws through each piece.

⑧ To encourage maximum use by butterflies throughout the year, place the box on a post 4 to 6 feet off the ground in a location that is partially shaded from direct sunlight and sheltered from strong winds. In this position, the box will be protected from extreme temperatures that would be uncomfortable for, or even harm, butterflies. Try to place the front of the box and the entrance slits facing east and south, the general direction of the sun, but not exposed to prevailing winds.

November

Region-by-Region Checklist

ZONES 2 AND 3 Walking over lawns and groundcovers once the ground has frozen can damage or even kill your plants, so stay on paths and walkways. Add additional mulch over perennial and annual beds when the ground freezes. Make sure all young trees are securely staked against winter gales. Check that tree guards are in place to prevent bark from being damaged by wildlife.

ZONE 4 Follow the activity checklist for Zones 2 and 3.

ZONE 5 Apply compost or another balanced organic fertilizer to lawns and ornamental grasses. Unless you plan to leave perennials in place over winter for wildlife, cut them down; pull out annuals when the foliage dies back and apply winter mulch over these areas. Apply winter mulch around trees and shrubs. Stake and wrap new trees and shrubs in burlap for winter protection.

ZONE 6 Apply compost or another balanced organic fertilizer to lawns and ornamental grasses. Unless you plan to leave perennials in place over winter for wildlife, cut them down; pull out annuals when the foliage dies back. Fertilize trees and shrubs. Stake and wrap trunks of new trees and shrubs.

ZONE 7 Set out bird feeders this month. Plant groundcovers and ornamental grasses. Lift and divide ornamental grasses that have become crowded and replant divisions. Deadhead perennials and annuals when their flowers fade. Plant and fertilize new trees and shrubs. Apply mulch around trees and shrubs.

ZONE 8 Follow the activity checklist for Zone 7.

ZONES 9 AND 10 Plant new groundcovers and ornamental grasses, and water as needed. Divide ornamental grasses that have become crowded and replant divisions. Plant new perennials and hardy annuals. Divide perennials that have become crowded and replant divisions. Plant new trees and shrubs and fertilize with compost or another balanced organic fertilizer.

PREPARE THE MINIPOND FOR WINTER

If you have a water garden, it doesn't take much to prepare your pond — and the fish and plants that live there — for the cold months to come.

If your minipond has no fish and the aquatic plant life has not become overgrown, there is not much work to do at all before winter. Just change some of the water and remove most of the leaves that have fallen into the pond. Then cover the minipond with a net to keep additional leaves from falling in the water.

If you have fish, you will definitely need to change about two-thirds of the water and remove all leaves, which, if left, will give off toxic gases as they decompose. If your water is chlorinated, you can't just add it straight from the hose. Make sure you let chlorine evaporate for at least three days before adding new water to your pond. You also will need to clean algae from the base of the minipond and cut back any plants, other than reeds or grasses, that are growing too vigorously. Add a mechanical deicer with an air pump to allow oxygen to permeate the water during winter before netting the pond, as described above.

Make a simple pond cover

Miniponds that have fish and are located in Zones 1 through 6 and in Maryland, Virginia and Delaware should be covered in winter. To make a simple cover, build a square frame from 2 × 2-inch lumber, with a few evenly spaced crosspieces. The frame should overlap the outside edges of the minipond by 2 feet all around. Cover the frame with heavy plastic sheeting or fiberglass-reinforced plastic attached to the wood with staples. The cover material must be transparent enough to allow sunlight to pass through.

Place the covered frame over the minipond and anchor the south end tightly to the ground with stakes or with heavy stones on top of it. Prop up the north end of the cover 6 to 8 inches with several stacks of bricks. Finally, anchor the elevated north end securely by placing bricks on top or by tying it down with a rope. There will be some snow build-up on the north side, but the south end generally stays open.

Winter is a trying time for those backyard habitat owners who include a minipond among their offerings to the critters. With just a bit of simple and inexpensive preparation, however, even small miniponds can come nicely through the most severe winters. Proper preparation can even leave the minipond available for wildlife during the winter.

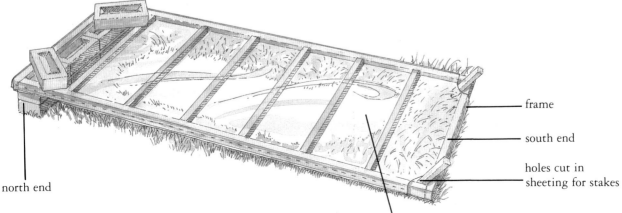

north end

frame

south end

holes cut in sheeting for stakes

heavy plastic sheeting

BUILD A WINTER
ROOSTING BOX FOR BIRDS

When winter temperatures fall steeply, provide your local bird population with a winter roosting box to help them survive the cold.

What you'll need

1-inch lumber, cut into:

    Two 32 × 9-inch side pieces

    One 30 × 10-inch front piece

    One 36 × 10-inch back piece

    One 8 × 9-inch floor piece

    One 3 × 6-inch porch piece

    One 11 × 12-inch roof piece

¾₆-inch dowel rod, cut into three

    9¾-inch sections

Twenty-two 2-inch wood screws

Four 1¾-inch wood screws

Two ½-inch wood screws

Two metal hinges

Wood glue

Here's what to do

1 Cut the top of each side at an angle so that a slanted top results. Drill three ¾₆-inch holes into each side.

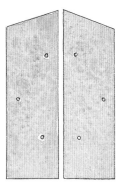

2 Cut a 2½ x 3-inch half-circle entrance hole in the bottom of the front.

3 Attach the back to the left side, aligning the bottom of the side with the bottom of the back so that the excess height of the back extends above the top of the side, using four 2-inch wood screws through the back into the side edge.

4 Attach the floor to the left side and back, using two 2-inch wood screws through both the side and back into the floor edge.

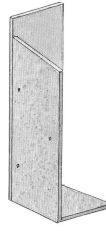

5 Apply wood glue around each of the three holes in the left side. Push one dowel rod into each hole, until it extends only ⅛-inch from the left side.

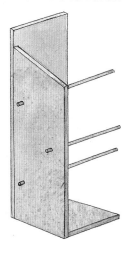

6 Attach the front to the edge of the left side using four 2-inch wood screws. Drive two 2-inch wood screws through the front into the floor.

7 Apply wood glue to the top of the porch and position it under the entrance hole so that 3 inches extend in front of the roosting box. Drive two 1¾-inch wood screws through the porch into the floor and two 1¾-inch wood screws through the floor into the porch.

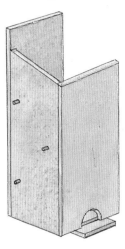

8 Apply wood glue to the three holes in the right side. Push the right side on to the dowel rods until the side is in position again relative to the back, front and floor. Attach them with four 2-inch wood screws through both the back and front into the side, and two 2-inch wood screws through the side into the floor.

9 Position the roof with an equal overhang on each side and an additional overhang in the front. Attach the roof to the back with two metal hinges. Secure the roof to the front with two ½-inch wood screws. These can be removed later to allow top access if needed.

10 Place the finished box on the trunk of a tree or post, from 8 to 10 feet above the ground, in a spot where it will receive full sun throughout the winter months but also will be protected from harsh winds. Use standard attachment devices, commonly available in hardware or nature stores.

BLACK-CAPPED
CHICKADEE
The dainty little black-capped chickadee is a common visitor to birdfeeders throughout the northern half of the country. It is particularly attracted to black oil-type sunflower seeds and suet.

MAKE YOUR FEEDERS SQUIRREL-PROOF

Outwitting squirrels has become a national pastime. The wily and voracious critters can wipe out your birdseed supplies in the blink of an eye.

The trick to keeping squirrels out of bird feeders is to keep them busy in their own feeding areas. Place a pile of field corn, bought at a bird supply store or gleaned (with permission) from a local farmer's field after his harvest, in some out-of-the-way corner of the backyard. This will divert much of the squirrels' attention and efforts away from the birdfeeders. You can also take this a stage further and install a feeder that makes the squirrels spend a considerable amount of time working out how to get each and every morsel (see "Construct a special squirrel feeder" on page 68).

Here's a tip from Leonard Lykens in Harrisburg, Pennsylvania: "When we bought our hanging birdfeeders, we also bought squirrel baffles, but we were outsmarted. The squirrel just went over the baffle, got into the feeder and enjoyed himself. After several tries at keeping the squirrel at bay, one trick seems to have worked. Using two squirrel baffles, I hung the first one the regular way (above the feeder, with the cup of the baffle pointing down toward the ground). Then I hung the second one upside down under the first, attaching it to the first with a piece of heavy wire from a coat hanger. I used the branch hook of the second baffle to hang the feeder.

"I do recommend that you drill two or three holes, about 1 inch from the center of the bottom baffle, to allow rainwater to drain away. This baffle plus an ample supply of sunflower seeds placed at the base of a big tree about once a week, seems to do the trick."

A recent development in the never-ending war on squirrels at backyard birdfeeders is special birdseed mixes that include cayenne pepper. The manufacturers of these products claim that the pepper repels the squirrels but does not harm the birds and is not detected by them. However, I remain unconvinced.

The only thing that's certain about squirrel-proof bird feeders is that not one of them, regardless of its design and extras, is really squirrel-proof.

KEEP DEER AT BAY

The white-tailed deer has become a common sight in the suburbs throughout much of the eastern United States in recent years. And, while these beautiful creatures are a pleasure to watch, they often wreak havoc on garden and landscape plants.

Usually the first few deer in a neighborhood are greeted as cute and special visitors. They are offered great quantities of food and, in general, find a place in the hearts of the community. But deer are prolific, and their numbers increase rapidly when not kept under control.

Soon the burgeoning deer population is eating expensive ornamental shrubs. Motorists are colliding with them on the roadways, doing extensive damage to the deer, the motor vehicle and often the psyche of the motorist. A few people may come down with Lyme disease, which is caused by a spirochete in ticks carried by the deer. At this point, the deer begin to lose their Bambi-ish appeal. Solutions to control their numbers are sought. Arguments over appropriate measures break out.

If you live in a suburb with a small amount of woodland in the eastern United States, your choice is not between attracting or repelling the deer. Your choice really becomes one of what – if any – areas of your property you are willing to allow the deer access to.

The only thing that ever has approached 100 percent effectiveness in repelling deer is an electrified fence. Opinions vary on the height of fence needed to keep out the deer, ranging anywhere from 6 to 9 feet. But as deer have been documented to jump more than 8 feet into the air with only normal effort, the 9-foot level would seem the better choice. Remember, too, that the

bottom of the fence must be firmly in contact with the ground along its entire length. Believe it or not, deer can crawl under barriers as well as jump over them.

Of course, few people want a 9-foot electrified fence all around their property, which brings me to other deer repellents. Basil, human hair, Zoo-Doo (manure from predators at the zoo), strongly scented deodorant soap, and an egg-water spray are some of the very best repellents.

Here's a tip: Change the repellent substance every other day and vary the locations of the repellents around the property. The one thing that doesn't scare a deer is something it's grown accustomed to and no longer senses as a threat. The repellents should be placed at several points along an imaginery border line around the plants to be protected.

In many areas across America, from suburban developments to city parks, populations of white-tailed deer are the most pressing issue facing those interested in or involved with wildlife. Deer populations have escalated in all protected locations where hunting, the usual method of control, can't reduce them.

MAKE A SUNFLOWER DECORATION FOR BIRDS

As autumn takes hold of the land, wreaths and other decorations of dried flowers are hung on doors, rails and fences. This beautiful arrangement is easy to make and will also benefit birds.

Use the large, dried seedhead from a sunflower plant to form the base of the decoration. Then, using light-gauge wire, attach dried stems of seedheads from various wildflowers, such as coneflowers, grasses and foxtails and domestic plants, such as wheat and sorghum. Small mesh sacks of suet or suet laced with birdseed can also be attached here and there. (See "Cook up recipes for the birds" on page 21.)

To finish the arrangement in a decorative fashion with human sensibilities in mind, add a bright ribbon and bow. The birds won't be put off by this final touch.

New uses for old decorations

When the colored Indian or strawberry corn decoration on your door or in your centerpiece for the Thanksgiving season begins to fade and lose its luster, don't just drop it into the garbage to make way for Christmas trimmings. Instead, give it to the wildlife. Critters will make use of it just as they do field corn. Crows, deer, raccoons and squirrels will take the kernels right off the cob. Chipmunks and jays will quickly clean up the kernels if you first remove them from the cob. With a bit of thought and creativity, many such common items can find new uses for wildlife.

While certain seeds are favored by most birds, almost any plant with a seedhead can be dried and used in a beautiful holiday display that will also benefit the critters.

KEEP YOUR EARS PEELED FOR OWLS

If your neighborhood has rodents and small birds, it almost certainly has predators like hawks and owls.

The easiest way to find and see owls is to listen for their calls. They begin calling from their daytime perch in early evening and continue into the night. Owls are often quite vocal during winter, and you should be able to home in on their position. If you don't make it all the way to their perch in one evening, remember your last position and begin there the following night.

Here are descriptions of the calls of three well-known owls that are widespread in the United States.

• The great horned owl produces the stereotypical owl hoot, which can carry over a deceptively long distance. Listen for its "whooo, who-who, whoo whoo," with the emphasis on the final two notes.

• The screech owl's call lives up to the bird's name, descending from high to low over the length of the note.

• The barn owl makes an alarming series of hisses, screams, clicks and grunts.

Now you know "who" it might be.

Three of the most common owl species across America are, from left, the great horned owl, the screech owl and the barn owl. Many more backyard habitat owners receive nighttime visits from these birds than ever realize it.

DECEMBER

REGION-BY-REGION CHECKLIST

ZONES 2 AND 3 If you haven't already done so, set out your birdseed and suet feeders and keep them filled through early spring. Walking on frozen groundcovers and lawn areas can cause damage or even kill plants, so stay on paths and walkways. Check your winter mulches regularly, and repair and replace as needed. Check to make sure wraps are in place on trees and shrubs. Make sure stakes supporting trees and shrubs are still firmly in the ground.

ZONE 4 Follow the activity checklist for Zones 2 and 3.

ZONE 5 Keep suet and seed feeders filled from now on. Your groundcover and lawn areas are now frozen; avoid walking on them, since this can damage or even kill plants. Check your mulches regularly, and repair and renew as needed.

ZONE 6 Follow the activity checklist for Zone 5.

ZONE 7 Set out birdfeeders this month if you haven't already done so. If groundcover and lawn areas freeze, avoid walking on them, since this can damage or even kill plants. Put down your winter mulches, begin checking them regularly, and repair and renew as needed. Before the ground freezes, water your new evergreens heavily.

ZONE 8 Set out birdfeeders this month if you haven't already done so. Put down winter mulches and renew as needed. You can extend the season for many perennials if you give them protective covering at night. Deadhead winter annuals when the flowers fade.

ZONES 9 AND 10 Feed your ornamental grasses and lawn areas with a light topdressing of compost. Plant new perennials and hardy annuals. Remove fall annuals and deadhead winter annuals when the flowers fade. Plant new trees and shrubs and water them deeply. Prune established trees, shrubs and vines.

PROTECT YOUR PLANTS DURING THE WINTER

Remember to take the needs of wildlife as well as your plants into consideration.

The fewer leaves and less autumn debris you remove from your flower beds and wildflower areas and from around your trees, shrubs and hedges, the easier time your plants will have during the winter months. Not only will the plants benefit from the protection of this natural blanket of mulch, but many creatures will also find shelter among the leaves and litter.

Of course, if you like a more manicured look, you may not want to leave much debris in place. If this is the case, you will need to add some insulating protection in the form of a mulch material like shredded bark that comes out of a bag. The level of nutrients in the mulch and debris provided naturally and freely by the environment will generally be higher, but the protection for the plants is about equal, and wildlife will find shelter in either type.

To protect shrubs and young trees from the harsh elements of winter, use burlap wraps. If at the same time you want to benefit wildlife, particularly the birds, cut several small holes about 3 inches in diameter into the burlap on the downwind side. In this way, you provide the equivalent of roosting boxes for the birds and, at the same time, protect the shrub or tree from the wind.

Similarly, stakes used to support the trees can also be used as wildlife-benefiting features. If the stakes are large enough, they can support bird feeders and roosting boxes.

Here's a tip about staking trees, although it has no importance for wildlife other than making sure the trees you plant for them survive. Don't make the tie between the tree and stake so tight that the tree can't sway slightly with the wind. If the tree can't move at all, it will fail to develop the flexibility it needs to survive many years of wind, and one day a strong wind will snap the trunk.

When ice or snow builds up on shrub or tree branches to the point of nearly snapping them off, there is no wildlife reason not to remove that buildup. So, for the benefit of the shrub or tree, gently brush the snow or ice from the branches. Never shake a frozen branch — it can easily break off in your hand.

A young tree needs some flexibility while it grows to enable it to deal with high winds and storms later in life. So when attaching a tree to a support stake, make sure that the tree is able to move slightly.

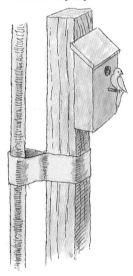

To protect your special shrubs and trees from the vagaries of winter while providing shelter for wildlife at the same time, cut several small holes in the downwind side of the wrap.

115

STOCK UP ON BIRDS' FAVORITE SEEDS

Some birds are more strongly attracted to certain seed types. Here are some general guidelines.

Birdseed	Birds attracted
Black-striped sunflower seed	Chipping sparrow, common flicker, common grackle, downy woodpecker, hairy woodpecker, purple finch, red-breasted nuthatch, scrub jay, song sparrow, tree sparrow, tufted titmouse, white-crowned sparrow
Cracked corn	Blue jay, Brewer's blackbird, brown-headed cowbird, common crow, common grackle, European starling, fox sparrow, house sparrow, mourning dove, red-winged blackbird, ring-necked pheasant, rufous-sided towhee, scrub jay, song sparrow, tree sparrow, white crowned sparrow, white-throated sparrow
Niger (or thistle) seed	American goldfinch, house finch, pine siskin
Oil-type sunflower seed	Black-capped chickadee, blue jay, Carolina chickadee, dark-eyed junco, house finch, mourning dove, northern cardinal, white-breasted nuthatch
Peanuts	Blue jay, gray catbird, scrub jay, tufted titmouse, white-throated sparrow
Safflower seed	Northern cardinal
White proso millet	Brewer's blackbird, fox sparrow, house finch, house sparrow, pine siskin, red-winged blackbird, song sparrow, tree sparrow, white-crowned sparrow, white-throated sparrow

chipping sparrow

blue jay

black-capped chickadee

northern cardinal

TRACK WILDLIFE IN WINTER

Where have all the critters gone? Although most of the wildlife may seem to have vanished, if you look around for tracks, you'll soon realize that plenty of birds and animals are still around.

Now that winter is here, insects, reptiles and amphibians are buried deep in the earth or under protective shelters. Many bird species have migrated to the South – or to Central and South America – although others are making their first backyard appearances after spending times of greater abundance in nearby woodlands. Even some of the mammals, including chipmunks, rabbits and groundhogs, have disappeared from the countryside. But there are still plenty of birds and other wildlife that you can enjoy in your winter habitat. And now's a great time to brush up on your track-identifying skills, especially when it snows.

If you haven't already done so, now is an excellent time of the year to start a backyard wildlife journal. See "Keep a 'guest book' for wildlife visitors" on page 20 for tips on how to proceed with this project. You'll deal with far fewer species than at other times of the year, but you'll probably observe the same individuals on a regular basis as they respond to the habitat elements you provide. Both of these circumstances will lead to a deeper understanding of individual creatures over a shorter time period than in the other seasons of the year.

With just a bit of practice and experience, you can find and identify tracks that reveal a great deal about wildlife.

See "Keep a 'guest book' for wildlife visitors" on page 20

TRACKS

Obtaining a field guide to animal tracks is a useful first step to identifying the critters. Wet snow, mud and dust are good conditions for finding clear prints.

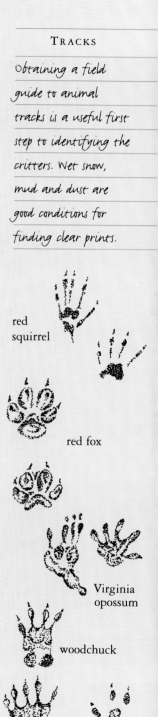

red
squirrel

red fox

Virginia
opossum

woodchuck

meadow vole

117

DECORATE A CHRISTMAS TREE FOR WILDLIFE

When you pick up your Christmas tree at the local lot this year, buy an extra one for the critters and deck it out with tasty treats for your birds and animals.

Position your wildlife Christmas tree in some convenient spot for viewing and secure it to the ground so it stays upright. If you already have a nicely shaped evergreen in your yard, you can decorate that instead and have a living Christmas tree. Just make sure it's easy to see from the house. In place of the lights, balls and silver tinsel you may use on your indoor tree, decorate the wildlife tree with edible ornaments. Here are some ideas.

Suet ornaments

The suet recipes given in "Cook up recipes for the birds" on page 21 can be used to make decorations. First prepare the recipe of your choice. Then, just as the suet mix is ready to solidify, dip pinecones and attractively twisted and bent twigs into the suet mix. Let the first coating dry, then dip the cones and twigs a second time. Repeat this process a half-dozen times. After the last coating has dried thoroughly, tie a string in a loop around one end of each cone and twig suet ornament.

To make a medallion, reheat the suet mix. Tie three toothpicks about 1 inch apart along one end of a string. Lay the toothpicks along the bottom of a small pan or the cut-off base of a large plastic soda bottle. Leave several inches of the other end of the string hanging out and

Wildlife Christmas trees can be made as simple or as elaborate as you want.

tied in a loop. Pour about ½-inch of the suet mix into the pan or soda-bottle base and allow it to solidify before turning it out of the pan. Repeat this process to make as many of these large, flat ornaments as you want.

Cornmeal cookies

The cornmeal recipe I told you about in "Cook up recipes for the birds" on page 22, can also be used now to make small, flat cookies. Simply mold your cookies into 1 inch-diameter rounds and press a length of string into each one. Form a loop for hanging from the bough of your tree. Bake as described in the recipe.

Strings and garlands

Take some strong sewing thread and cut it into 1 foot lengths. Then, leaving at least 2 inches free to form a loop, string on any combination of the following: cranberries, peanuts in the shell, sunflower seeds, large bread crumbs, or popped popcorn. This will give you small stringlike ornaments. To make garlands, follow the same procedure, but use 5 or 6 foot lengths of thread.

Fruit slices

You can hang orange and apple rounds on your tree, too. Just thread a string through the top and tie to make a hanging loop.

Finishing touches

For an added festive feel for your tree, add a few bright plastic bows and maybe some of your old Christmas balls. These additions can really set the tree off, particularly if you plan to take photos of it for your next year's Christmas cards; see "Make your own backyard Christmas cards" on page 121.

see "Make your own backyard Christmas cards" on page 121.

MAKE A YULE LOG

Take this holiday tradition into the outdoors for wildlife to enjoy by decorating the log with enticing tidbits.

To make a Yule log for wildlife, select a log at least 8 inches in diameter and 2 or more feet long. A white birch log is an attractive choice. Leave the bark in place. Drill several holes 2 inches in diameter and 2 inches deep, along the length and around the sides of the log.

Pack each of the holes with various suet and peanut butter mixes — see "Cook up recipes for the birds" on page 22. Make a few garlands of cranberries, popcorn and peanuts, just as you did for the Wildlife Christmas tree (opposite) and wrap them around the log. Add a few small pine boughs. Attach a bright plastic ribbon, and you're ready.

The log can be laid on its side on the ground, deck, porch or feeding station. Or it can be stood upright, supported by a pole, post or tree trunk. Fix the log firmly in place using a stake and wire.

Your backyard wildlife habitat can become an important and exciting part of the holiday season.

FLYING SQUIRREL

The flying squirrel is a regular visitor to feeders offering suet, seeds and mixes of the two. Mostly, the homeowner is completely unaware of its nighttime presence. The small squirrel glides rather than flies.

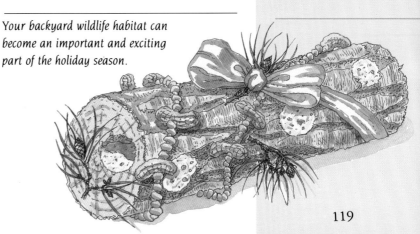

MAKE A CHRISTMAS WREATH WITH BIRDS IN MIND

Make a special holiday wreath to hang on your back door or on a nearby tree trunk. If you use
a mix of attractive seedheads, your design will be both decorative and appealing to the birds.

Start collecting material for your bird wreath during the fall. You can gather wildflower seedheads on their stems locally and dry them. Alternatively you may have also grown some wildflowers that form seedheads, like coneflowers, or have even planted a birdseed garden (see page 88), and dried their seedheads and stems. Or, you can buy dried seedheads of flowers and ornamental grasses at nurseries, nature stores, florists and craft stores. (If you buy seedheads, make sure they're untreated.)

What you'll need

One 12- to 16-inch straw wreath
    base
Any of the following:
    Small sunflower seedheads
    Bittersweet branches
    Sprays of rosehips
    Purple coneflower seedheads
    Black-eyed Susan seedheads
    Ornamental grass seedheads
    Wheat, rye or barley seedheads
    Safflower seedheads
    Strawberry corn (on the cob)
Floral picks
Floral pins
Medium-gauge-floral wire

Here's what to do

Pick a starting point on the straw wreath base and cover the entire surface of the wreath with some of the seedheads you've selected. Attach each seedhead to the wreath with a floral pick or floral pin, also available from florists and craft or hobby stores. Move along the straw wreath base and repeat this process again, overlapping most of the stems from the first row of seedheads with a second row. Continue this process all around the wreath until it is completely covered.

Cut a length of medium-gauge floral wire to use as a hanger. Twist it around what you've determined to be the top of your wreath.

MAKE YOUR OWN BACKYARD CHRISTMAS CARDS

Take a new look at your wildlife photos and turn the best into a personal greeting that your friends and family will treasure.

If you followed my advice in "Take a close-up look at wildlife" on page 92 about using blinds and taking better photos of your backyard critters, and particularly if you combined those ideas with the wildlife Christmas tree on page 118, you probably have some very artistic photos of some of your favorite creatures on hand. Look through them and consider which of them would look good printed on the front of this year's Christmas cards.

ASSESS THE PAST YEAR AND PLAN AHEAD

Look back over the past year in your backyard wildlife habitat, and answer the following questions before you make decisions for the next year.

Ask yourself these four questions as you think back over the year in your yard:

• Did the wildlife you hoped to attract respond to your efforts? What new wildlife would you like to attract next year? Remember that they must be ones that already live in your area. But, if you weren't able to attract a particular creature which you know inhabits your locality, learn how it meets its need for food, water, shelter and cover, as explained in "What is a niche?" on page 16. Then plan to make sure all four elements are in your yard next year.

• Were the plants you tried to grow this year successful? What new plants would you like to add next year? Again, if things went wrong, try to determine what happened by checking through this book and referring to a detailed plant guide.

• Were you happy with the special features – the birdfeeders, nestboxes and trails – ? If so, what new features would you like to add next year?

• Finally, what happened in your habitat that pleased you most? Can you do anything to make sure it happens again next year?

DIRECTORY OF PLANTS FOR WILDLIFE GARDENS

Coming up with a list of "best" plants for use in backyard wildlife habitats is much like telling someone what the "best" flavor of ice cream is for them when they're looking at a selection of dozens of flavors. I can't tell you what you'll like. But I can show you 100 of the very best trees, shrubs, annuals, perennials, vines, groundcovers, and grasses for wildlife. Then you can use this directory as a starting point to narrow down the selections or to gather ideas for your own property.

This is a very special list of plants. Not only do these plants offer a lot for the critters, but they also will bring beauty into the backyard. In making these selections, I never lost sight of the use to which these plants are being put. They are not only food, cover and shelter for the critters, but they also

must be outstanding plants for the home landscape. They must produce foliage, flowers, fruit, fall color and other ornamental features of which you can be proud.

Finally, they must be readily available to you through gardening catalogs and your local nurseries and garden centers. Knowing the value of a particular plant and wanting to grow that plant on your property is of very little use if you can't obtain that plant. You will be able to find all these plants through your regular sources.

I've collected the plants, told you how to grow and use them, and included what kinds of critters each plant will attract. Now it's your turn to page through the directory, pick your favorites, and get ready to welcome wildlife to your backyard habitat.

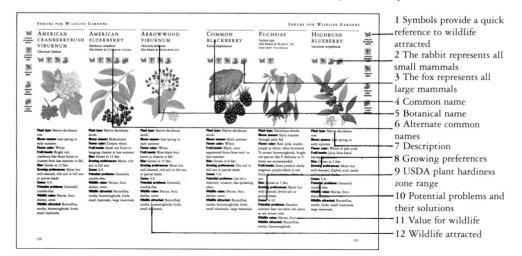

1 Symbols provide a quick reference to wildlife attracted

2 The rabbit represents all small mammals

3 The fox represents all large mammals

4 Common name

5 Botanical name

6 Alternate common names

7 Description

8 Growing preferences

9 USDA plant hardiness zone range

10 Potential problems and their solutions

11 Value for wildlife

12 Wildlife attracted

ALLEGHENY SERVICEBERRY

Amelanchier laevis

Plant type: Native deciduous tree.
Bloom season: Spring.
Flower color: White.
Fruit/seeds: Pulpy black fruits from summer into fall.
Size: Grows to 20 feet.
Growing preferences: Moist but well-drained, neutral to slightly acid soil in a sunny location.
Zones: 4-8.
Potential problems: Fireblight is sometimes a problem.
Wildlife value: Nectar, fruit, shelter, cover.
Wildlife attracted: Butterflies, moths, birds, small mammals.

AMERICAN HOLLY

Ilex opaca

Plant type: Native evergreen tree
Bloom season: Spring.
Flower color: White.
Fruit/seeds: Red berries from fall into winter.
Size: Grows to 45 feet.
Growing preferences: Well-drained soil in sun or shade. Does not grow well in coastal areas.
Zones: 6-9.
Potential problems: For reliable fruiting, plant both male and female trees in close proximity. Responds to heavy pruning but does not transplant well.
Wildlife value: Nectar, fruit, shelter, cover.
Wildlife attracted: Butterflies, moths, birds, small mammals.

AMERICAN MOUNTAIN ASH

Sorbus americana

Plant type: Native deciduous tree.
Bloom season: Early summer.
Flower color: White.
Fruit/seeds: Red fruits in early fall.
Size: Grows to 30 feet.
Growing preferences: Moist but well-drained soil of high fertility in full sun or partial shade.
Zones: 5-8
Potential problems: Fireblight.
Wildlife value: Nectar, fruit, shelter, cover.
Wildlife attracted: Butterflies, moths, birds, small mammals.

ATTRACTS BUTTERFLIES/ MOTHS

ATTRACTS HUMMINGBIRDS

ATTRACTS BIRDS

ATTRACTS SMALL MAMMALS

ATTRACTS LARGE MAMMALS

AMERICAN PLANETREE

Platanus occidentalis
Also known as BUTTONWOOD *or*
AMERICAN SYCAMORE

Plant type: Native deciduous tree.
Bloom season: Spring.
Flower color: Yellowish.
Fruit/seeds: Ball-like structure holding nutlets through the winter.
Size: Grows to 110 feet.
Growing preferences: Moist, acid soil in full sun.
Zones: 4-7.
Potential problems: Generally trouble-free.
Wildlife value: Nectar, nutlets, shelter, cover.
Wildlife attracted: Butterflies, moths, hummingbirds, birds, small mammals, large mammals.

BALSAM FIR

Abies balsamea

Plant type: Native evergreen coniferous tree.
Fruit/seeds: Cones.
Size: Grows to 75 feet.
Growing preferences: Moist, slightly acid soil in partial shade.
Zones: 4-7.
Potential problems: Young trees may need protection from winter wind, ice and snow.
Wildlife value: Sap, cones, shelter, cover.
Wildlife attracted: Birds, small mammals, large mammals.

CANADA HEMLOCK

Tsuga canadensis

Plant type: Native evergreen coniferous tree.
Fruit/seeds: Cones.
Size: Grows to 75 feet.
Growing preferences: Moist, acid soil in partial shade.
Zones: 3-8.
Potential problems: Woolly adelgids.
Wildlife value: Cones, shelter, cover.
Wildlife attracted: Birds, small mammals.

CHOKECHERRY

Prunus virginiana
Also known as VIRGINIA BIRD CHERRY

Plant type: Native deciduous tree.
Bloom season: Mid- to late-spring.
Flower color: White.
Fruit/seeds: Red fruits in summer mature to purple.
Size: Grows to 30 feet.
Growing preferences: Moist but well-drained soil in full sun.
Zones: 3-8.
Potential problems: Aphids, silver leaf disease, witches' broom fungus.
Wildlife value: Nectar, fruit, shelter, cover.
Wildlife attracted: Butterflies, moths, hummingbirds, birds, small mammals, large mammals.

COCKSPUR HAWTHORN

Crataegus crus-galli

Plant type: Native deciduous tree.
Bloom season: Late spring.
Flower color: White petals with pink-tipped stamens.
Fruit/seeds: Bright red fruits from summer through fall.
Size: Grows to 25 feet.
Growing preferences: Adaptable to a wide range of soil conditions, except continuously wet soils. Prefers full sun.
Zones: 4-7.
Potential problems: Fireblight is sometimes a problem.
Wildlife value: Nectar, fruit, shelter, cover.
Wildlife attracted: Butterflies, moths, birds, small mammals, large mammals.

COLORADO SPRUCE

Picea pungens
Also known as COLORADO BLUE SPRUCE

Plant type: Native evergreen coniferous tree.
Fruit/seeds: Cones.
Size: Grows to 50 feet.
Growing preferences: Moist, well-drained, rich soil in full sun. Plants are drought-tolerant.
Zones: 3-7.
Potential problems: Generally trouble-free.
Wildlife value: Cones, shelter, cover.
Wildlife attracted: Birds, small mammals, large mammals.

ATTRACTS BUTTERFLIES/ MOTHS

ATTRACTS HUMMING-BIRDS

ATTRACTS BIRDS

ATTRACTS SMALL MAMMALS

ATTRACTS LARGE MAMMALS

ATTRACTS
BUTTERFLIES/
MOTHS

ATTRACTS
HUMMING-
BIRDS

ATTRACTS
BIRDS

ATTRACTS
SMALL
MAMMALS

ATTRACTS
LARGE
MAMMALS

COMMON HACKBERRY

Celtis occidentalis
Also known as NETTLE TREE

Plant type: Native deciduous tree.

Bloom season: Spring.

Flower color: White.

Fruit/seeds: Fruits are bright green, turning yellowish red, then purplish red in fall.

Size: Grows to 70 feet.

Growing preferences: Well-drained, fertile soil in full sun.

Zones: 2-9.

Potential problems: Generally trouble-free. Leaf galls may be a problem.

Wildlife value: Nectar, fruit, shelter, cover.

Wildlife attracted: Butterflies, moths, birds, small mammals.

EASTERN RED CEDAR

Juniperus virginiana

Plant type: Native evergreen coniferous tree.

Fruit/seeds: Blue-green berries from late summer to fall.

Size: Grows to 70 feet.

Growing preferences: Moist but well-drained, rich to average soil in full sun.

Zones: 6-9.

Potential problems: Generally trouble-free.

Wildlife value: Fruit, shelter, cover.

Wildlife attracted: Birds, small mammals, large mammals.

EASTERN WHITE PINE

Pinus strobus
Also known as WHITE PINE

Plant type: Native evergreen coniferous tree.

Fruit/seeds: Cones.

Size: Grows to 80 feet.

Growing preferences: Moist, rich to average soil in full sun.

Zones: 3-9.

Potential problems: Generally trouble-free.

Wildlife value: Cones, shelter, cover.

Wildlife attracted: Birds, small mammals, large mammals.

FLOWERING DOGWOOD

Cornus florida

Plant type: Native deciduous tree.

Bloom season: Late spring.

Flower color: White or pink.

Fruit/seeds: Orange-red berries in fall.

Size: Grows to 20 feet.

Growing preferences: Moist but well-drained, rich to average soil in partial or light shade.

Zone: 5-9

Potential problems: Anthracnose leaf disease.

Wildlife value: Nectar, fruit, shelter, cover.

Wildlife attracted: Butterflies, moths, hummingbirds, birds, small mammals.

PIN CHERRY

Prunus pensylvanica

Plant type: Native deciduous tree.

Bloom season: Mid- to late-spring.

Flower color: White.

Fruit/seeds: Small red fruits in summer.

Size: Grows to 50 feet.

Growing preferences: Adaptable to a wide range of soil conditions, except constantly wet soil. Prefers full sun.

Zones: 3-8.

Potential problems: Aphids, silver leaf fungus, witches' broom fungus.

Wildlife value: Nectar, fruit, shelter, cover.

Wildlife attracted: Butterflies, moths, hummingbirds, birds, small mammals.

RED MULBERRY

Morus rubra

Plant type: Native deciduous tree.

Bloom season: Spring.

Flower color: White.

Fruit/seeds: Fleshy red fruits in summer.

Size: Grows to 40 feet.

Growing preferences: Moist but well-drained, fertile soil in full sun.

Zones: 5-9.

Potential problems: Generally trouble-free.

Wildlife value: Nectar, fruit, shelter, cover.

Wildlife attracted: Butterflies, moths, hummingbirds, birds, small mammals.

ATTRACTS BUTTERFLIES/ MOTHS

ATTRACTS HUMMING- BIRDS

ATTRACTS BIRDS

ATTRACTS SMALL MAMMALS

ATTRACTS LARGE MAMMALS

RIVER BIRCH

Betula nigra
Also known as BLACK BIRCH *or*
RED BIRCH

Plant type: Native deciduous
tree.
Bloom season: Spring.
Flower color: Catkins are dark
brown.
Fruit/seeds: Nutlets borne in tan
catkins in spring.
Size: Grows to 45 feet.
Propagation: Moist but well-
drained, slightly acid soil in full
sun to partial shade.
Zones: 4-9
Potential problems: Generally
trouble-free.
Wildlife value: Catkins, shelter,
cover.
Wildlife attracted: Butterflies,
moths, birds, small mammals,
large mammals.

RUSSIAN OLIVE

Elaeagnus angustifolia

Plant type: Deciduous tree.
Bloom season: Early summer.
Flower color: Yellow.
Fruit/seeds: Yellow fruits in late
summer.
Size: Grows to 20 feet.
Growing preferences: Well-
drained, fertile soil in full sun.
Zones: 2-9.
Potential problems: Generally
trouble-free.
Wildlife value: Nectar, fruit,
shelter, cover.
Wildlife attracted: Butterflies,
moths, birds, small mammals,
large mammals.

SMOOTH ALDER

Alnus rugosa
Also known as STREAM ALDER

Plant type: Native deciduous
tree.
Bloom season: Late winter to
early spring.
Flower color: Yellowish green.
Fruit/seeds: Catkins from late
winter to early spring.
Size: Grows to 15 feet.
Growing preferences: Wet, acid
soil in full sun to partial shade.
Zones: 4-7.
Potential problems: Generally
trouble-free.
Wildlife value: Catkins, shelter,
cover.
Wildlife attracted: Birds, small
mammals.

WHITE OAK

Quercus alba

Plant type: Native deciduous tree.
Bloom season: Late spring to early summer.
Flower color: Pale green.
Fruit/seeds: Acorns from late summer through fall.
Size: Grows to 60 feet.
Growing preferences: Well-drained, average soil in full sun.
Zones: 5-9.
Potential problems: Mildew, oak galls, oak wilt.
Wildlife value: Nuts, shelter, cover.
Wildlife attracted: Birds, small mammals, large mammals.

WILD CRABAPPLE

Malus coronaria

Plant type: Native deciduous tree.
Bloom season: Spring.
Flower color: Pink or white.
Fruit/seeds: Small yellowish apples from late summer into fall.
Size: Grows to 25 feet.
Growing preferences: Moist but well-drained, rich soil in full sun.
Zones: 3-8.
Potential problems: Aphids, red spider mites, fireblight, apple scab.
Wildlife value: Nectar, fruit, shelter, cover.
Wildlife attracted: Butterflies, moths, hummingbirds, birds, small mammals, large mammals.

WILLOWS

Salix spp.

Plant type: Native deciduous trees.
Bloom season: Spring.
Flower color: Yellowish green.
Fruit/seeds: Yellowish catkins in spring.
Size: Grows to 70 feet.
Growing preferences: Adaptable to a wide range of soil conditions, except very dry soil. Prefers full sun.
Zones: 4-9.
Potential problems: Aphids, gall mites, fungal diseases. A messy plant that drops a nearly constant supply of litter.
Wildlife value: Catkins, shelter, cover.
Wildlife attracted: Birds, small mammals.

ATTRACTS BUTTERFLIES/MOTHS

ATTRACTS HUMMINGBIRDS

ATTRACTS BIRDS

ATTRACTS SMALL MAMMALS

ATTRACTS LARGE MAMMALS

ATTRACTS BUTTERFLIES/ MOTHS

ATTRACTS HUMMING- BIRDS

ATTRACTS BIRDS

ATTRACTS SMALL MAMMALS

ATTRACTS LARGE MAMMALS

AMERICAN CRANBERRYBUSH VIBURNUM

Viburnum trilobum

Plant type: Native deciduous tree.

Bloom season: Late spring to early summer.

Flower color: White.

Fruit/seeds: Bright red, cranberry-like fruits borne in clusters from late summer to fall.

Size: Grows to 12 feet.

Growing preferences: Moist but well-drained, rich soil in full sun or partial shade.

Zones: 4-9.

Potential problems: Generally trouble-free.

Wildlife value: Nectar, fruit, shelter, cover.

Wildlife attracted: Butterflies, moths, hummingbirds, birds, small mammals.

AMERICAN ELDERBERRY

Sambucus canadensis
Also known as COMMON ELDER

Plant type: Native deciduous shrub.

Bloom season: Midsummer.

Flower color: Creamy white.

Fruit/seeds: Small red fruits in hanging clusters in late summer.

Size: Grows to 12 feet.

Growing preferences: Moist, rich soil in full sun.

Zones: 4-9.

Potential problems: Generally trouble-free.

Wildlife value: Nectar, fruit, shelter, cover.

Wildlife attracted: Butterflies, moths, hummingbirds, birds, small mammals, large mammals.

ARROWWOOD VIBURNUM

Viburnum dentatum
Also known as ARROWWOOD

Plant type: Native deciduous shrub.

Bloom season: Late spring to early summer.

Flower color: White.

Fruit/seeds: Blue-black fruit borne in clusters in fall.

Size: Grows to 15 feet.

Growing preferences: Moist but well-drained, rich soil in full sun or partial shade.

Zones: 4-9.

Potential problems: Generally trouble-free.

Wildlife value: Nectar, fruit, shelter, cover.

Wildlife attracted: Butterflies, moths, hummingbirds, birds, small mammals.

COMMON BLACKBERRY

Rubus alleghheniensis

Plant type: Native deciduous shrub.
Bloom season: Early summer.
Flower color: White.
Fruit/seeds: Black, juicy segmented fruits from mid- to late-summer.
Size: Grows to 8 feet.
Growing preferences: Dry soil in full sun or partial shade.
Zones: 5-9.
Potential problems: Can be a relatively invasive, fast-spreading plant.
Wildlife value: Nectar, fruit, shelter, cover.
Wildlife attracted: Butterflies, moths, hummingbirds, birds, small mammals, large mammals.

FUCHSIAS

Fuchsia spp.
Also known as HARDY OR SHRUBBY FUCHSIAS

Plant type: Deciduous shrubs.
Bloom season: Early summer through early fall.
Flower color: Red, pink, scarlet, purple or white; often bicolored. To attract hummingbirds, bright red species like *F. boliviana* or *F. brutus* are recommended.
Fruit/seeds: Some produce shady magenta, purple-black or red fruits in late summer; others do not.
Size: Grows to 5 feet.
Growing preferences: Moist but well-drained, fertile soil in partial shade.
Zones: 4-10.
Potential problems: Extreme summer heat can harm the plant, as can winter cold.
Wildlife value: Nectar, fruit.
Wildlife attracted: Butterflies, moths, hummingbirds.

HIGHBUSH BLUEBERRY

Vaccinium corymbosum

Plant type: Native deciduous tree.
Bloom season: Late spring to early summer.
Flower color: White or pale pink.
Fruit/seeds: Juicy blue-black berries in summer.
Size: Grows to 5 feet.
Growing preferences: Moist but well-drained, slightly acid, sandy soil in partial shade.
Zones: 5-8.
Potential problems: Generally trouble-free.
Wildlife value: Nectar, fruit, shelter, cover.
Wildlife attracted: Butterflies, moths, birds, small mammals, large mammals.

ATTRACTS BUTTERFLIES/ MOTHS

ATTRACTS HUMMING- BIRDS

ATTRACTS BIRDS

ATTRACTS SMALL MAMMALS

ATTRACTS LARGE MAMMALS

ATTRACTS
BUTTERFLIES/
MOTHS

ATTRACTS
HUMMING-
BIRDS

ATTRACTS
BIRDS

ATTRACTS
SMALL
MAMMALS

ATTRACTS
LARGE
MAMMALS

LEMON BOTTLEBRUSH

Callistemon citrinus
Also known as BOTTLEBRUSH BUSH

Plant type: Deciduous shrub.
Bloom season: Early summer.
Flower color: Red or yellow, depending on the cultivar, in bottlebrush-like spikes. Red-flowering cultivars, such as 'Splendens', are recommended for attracting hummingbirds.
Fruit/seeds: Insignificant capsule-like fruits in buttonlike clusters.
Size: Grows to 10 feet.
Growing preferences: Moist but well-drained, fertile soil in full sun.
Zones: 8-10.
Potential problems: When grown in Zone 8, the plant needs protection from the wind and cold.
Wildlife value: Nectar, shelter, cover.
Wildlife attracted: Butterflies, moths, hummingbirds, birds.

LILACS

Syringa spp.

Plant type: Deciduous shrubs.
Bloom season: Late spring through early summer.
Flower color: Lilac, white, mauve, purple or pink. 'Belle de Nancy' and 'Souvenir de Louis Spath' attract hummingbirds.
Fruit/seeds: Insignificant capsules.
Size: Grows to 15 feet.
Growing preferences: Well-drained, fertile, slightly alkaline soil in full sun.
Zones: 4-8, though some cultivars will grow as far north as Zone 3.
Potential problems: Powdery mildew, lilac blight, leaf spot, leaf miners.
Wildlife value: Nectar, shelter, cover.
Wildlife attracted: Butterflies, moths, hummingbirds, birds, small mammals.

OCOTILLO

Fouquieria splendens

Plant type: Native cactus-like shrub.
Bloom season: Summer.
Flower color: Red.
Fruit/seeds: Capsule that splits open to reveal dry, papery seeds.
Size: Grows to 20 feet.
Growing preferences: Dry, well-drained soil in full sun.
Zones: 8-10.
Potential problems: Leafless when not watered regularly.
Wildlife value: Nectar, shelter, cover.
Wildlife attracted: Butterflies, moths, hummingbirds.

ORANGE-EYE BUTTERFLY BUSH

Buddleia davidii
Also known as BUTTERFLY BUSH

Plant type: Native deciduous shrub.
Bloom season: Midsummer through fall.
Flower color: Violet-purple.
Fruit/seeds: Insignificant capsules.
Size: Grows to 15 feet.
Growing preferences: Well-drained, fertile soil in full sun.
Zones: 5-9.
Potential problems: Needs to be pruned back hard in late winter each year to promote new growth, since blooms are borne on new growth. Susceptible to freezing out.
Wildlife value: Nectar.
Wildlife attracted: Butterflies, moths, hummingbirds.

RED-OSIER DOGWOOD

Cornus sericea

Plant type: Native deciduous shrub.
Bloom season: Late spring to early summer.
Flower color: White.
Fruit/seeds: White to blue globular fruits from late summer into fall.
Size: Grows to 10 feet.
Growing preferences: Well-drained, fertile soil in full sun or partial shade.
Zones: 3-8.
Potential problems: Generally trouble-free.
Wildlife value: Nectar, shelter, cover, fruit.
Wildlife attracted: Butterflies, moths, hummingbirds, birds, small mammals, large mammals.

RHODODENDRONS AND AZALEAS

Rhododendron spp.

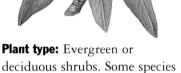

Plant type: Evergreen or deciduous shrubs. Some species are native.
Bloom season: Early spring into summer, depending on the species and cultivar.
Flower color: Red, pink, purple, orange, yellow or white.
Fruit/seeds: Insignificant capsules.
Size: Grows to 20 feet.
Growing preferences: Well-drained, fertile, acid soil in partial shade.
Zones: 5-9.
Potential problems: Weevils, powdery mildew. Easily damaged by poor drainage.
Wildlife value: Nectar, shelter, cover.
Wildlife attracted: Butterflies, moths, hummingbirds, birds, small mammals, large mammals.

ATTRACTS
BUTTERFLIES/
MOTHS

ATTRACTS
HUMMING-
BIRDS

ATTRACTS
BIRDS

ATTRACTS
SMALL
MAMMALS

ATTRACTS
LARGE
MAMMALS

ATTRACTS BUTTERFLIES/ MOTHS

ATTRACTS HUMMING- BIRDS

ATTRACTS BIRDS

ATTRACTS SMALL MAMMALS

ATTRACTS LARGE MAMMALS

RUGOSA ROSE

Rosa rugosa

Plant type: Non-native deciduous shrub.
Bloom season: Spring into summer.
Flower color: White, pink, rose or mauve.
Fruit/seeds: Large red hips from fall into winter.
Size: Grows to 6 feet.
Growing preferences: Well-drained soil in a sunny location.
Zones: 2-7.
Potential problems: Generally trouble-free.
Wildlife value: Fruit, shelter, cover.
Wildlife attracted: Birds, small mammals.

SCARLET FIRETHORN

Pyracantha coccinea
Also known as PYRACANTHA *or* FIRETHORN

Plant type: Evergreen shrub.
Bloom season: Summer.
Flower color: White.
Fruit/seeds: Spherical red, orange or yellow fruits in late summer.
Size: Grows to 15 feet.
Growing preferences: Well-drained, fertile soil in partial shade with protection from cold winds.
Zones: 6-9.
Potential problems: Fireblight, scab.
Wildlife value: Nectar, fruit, shelter, cover.
Wildlife attracted: Butterflies, moths, hummingbirds, birds, small mammals.

SHRIMP PLANT

Justicia brandegeano,
formerly Beloperone guttata

Plant type: Evergreen shrub.
Bloom season: Summer.
Flower color: White with red bracts.
Fruit/seeds: Insignificant capsules.
Size: Grows to 5 feet.
Growing preferences: Well-drained, fertile soil in full sun.
Zones: 8-10.
Potential problems: Whiteflies.
Wildlife value: Nectar, shelter, cover.
Wildlife attracted: Butterflies, moths, hummingbirds, birds, small mammals.

STAGHORN SUMAC

Rhus typhina

Plant type: Native deciduous shrub.

Bloom season: Mid- to late-summer.

Flower color: Greenish white.

Fruit/seeds: Red fruits borne in clusters in fall. Only female plants bear fruit.

Size: Grows to 15 feet.

Growing preferences: Well-drained soil in full sun to partial shade.

Zones: 3-8.

Potential problems: Coral spot fungus.

Wildlife value: Nectar, fruit, shelter, cover.

Wildlife attracted: Butterflies, moths, hummingbirds, birds, small mammals, large mammals.

WAX MYRTLE

Myrica cerifera
Also known as BAYBERRY

Plant type: Native evergreen shrub.

Bloom season: Summer into fall.

Flower color: White.

Fruit/seeds: Blue-black berries in fall.

Size: Grows to 15 feet.

Growing preferences: Moist but well-drained, fertile soil in full sun.

Zones: 8-9.

Potential problems: Requires winter protection in Zone 7. In more northerly climates (Zones 3-6), grow wax myrtle's deciduous relative, northern bayberry (*Myrica pensylvanica*), which bears fragrant clusters of waxy, gray berries.

Wildlife value: Nectar, fruit, shelter, cover.

Wildlife attracted: Butterflies, moths, hummingbirds, birds, small mammals.

WINTERBERRY

Ilex verticillata

Plant type: Native deciduous shrub.

Bloom season: Spring.

Flower color: White.

Fruit/seeds: Red berries from fall through winter.

Size: Grows to 6 feet.

Growing preferences: Well-drained soil in full sun or partial shade.

Zones: 4-9.

Potential problems: Holly leafminer, holly aphid.

Wildlife value: Nectar, fruit, shelter, cover.

Wildlife attracted: Butterflies, moths, hummingbirds, birds, small mammals, large mammals.

ATTRACTS BUTTERFLIES/ MOTHS

ATTRACTS HUMMING-BIRDS

ATTRACTS BIRDS

ATTRACTS SMALL MAMMALS

ATTRACTS LARGE MAMMALS

ATTRACTS
BUTTERFLIES/
MOTHS

ATTRACTS
HUMMING-
BIRDS

ATTRACTS
BIRDS

ATTRACTS
SMALL
MAMMALS

ATTRACTS
LARGE
MAMMALS

CARDINAL CLIMBER

Ipomoea quamoclit
Also known as CYPRESS VINE

Plant type: Native deciduous vine.

Bloom season: Summer.

Flower color: Bright red.

Fruit/seeds: Bright blue berries in fall.

Size: Grows to 10 feet.

Growing preferences: Well-drained, fertile soil in full sun with upright support provided. Roots need to be mulched or otherwise shaded from the sun.

Zones: 8-10. Plant can be grown as an annual north of Zone 8.

Potential problems: Whiteflies, red spider mites.

Wildlife value: Nectar, fruit, shelter, cover.

Wildlife attracted: Butterflies, moths, hummingbirds, birds, small mammals, large mammals.

CROSS VINE

Bignonia capreolata
Also known as TRUMPET FLOWER

Plant type: Evergreen to semi-evergreen vine.

Bloom season: Summer.

Flower color: Reddish orange, borne in clusters.

Fruit/seeds: Pea pod-like fruit in fall.

Size: Grows to 30 feet.

Growing preferences: Well-drained, fertile soil in full sun.

Zones: 6-10.

Potential problems: May drop leaves in areas with cold winter temperatures.

Wildlife value: Nectar, fruit, shelter, cover.

Wildlife attracted: Butterflies, moths, hummingbirds, birds.

FOX GRAPE

Vitis vulpina
Also known as RIVERSIDE GRAPE, FROST GRAPE *and* CHICKEN GRAPE

Plant type: Native deciduous vine.

Bloom season: Summer.

Flower color: Insignificant greenish flowers.

Fruit/seeds: Blue-black fruit in clusters in late summer to fall.

Size: Grows to 25 feet.

Growing preferences: Well-drained, fertile, coarse soil in partial shade.

Zones: 5-9.

Potential problems: The fruits can be very messy.

Wildlife value: Fruit.

Wildlife attracted: Butterflies, moths, hummingbirds, birds, small mammals, large mammals.

TRUMPET HONEYSUCKLE

Lonicera sempervirens
Also known as CORAL HONEYSUCKLE

Plant type: Native deciduous or evergreen vine.
Bloom season: Summer.
Flower color: Red to orange with yellow throats, borne in hanging clusters.
Fruit/seeds: Orange or scarlet berries.
Size: Grows to 12 feet.
Growing preferences: Well-drained, fertile soil in partial shade.
Zones: 4-9. Evergreen in Zones 8 and 9.
Potential problems: Aphids.
Wildlife value: Nectar, shelter, cover, fruit.
Wildlife attracted: Butterflies, moths, hummingbirds, birds, small mammals.

TRUMPET VINE

Campsis radicans
Also known as TRUMPET CREEPER

Plant type: Native deciduous vine.
Bloom season: Late summer into early fall.
Flower color: Red, orange or yellow flowers, borne in clusters.
Fruit/seeds: Insignificant capsule.
Size: Grows to 40 feet.
Growing preferences: Well-drained, fertile soil in full sun, with regular watering.
Zones: 5-9.
Potential problems: Generally trouble-free.
Wildlife value: Nectar.
Wildlife attracted: Butterflies, moths, hummingbirds.

VIRGINIA CREEPER

Parthenocissus quinquefolia
Also known as FIVE-LEAVED IVY

Plant type: Native deciduous vine.
Bloom season: Summer.
Flower color: Insignificant greenish flowers.
Fruit/seeds: Blue-black berries in fall.
Size: Grows to 50 feet.
Growing preferences: Well-drained soil in partial shade with strong, large trellis or other vertical support.
Zones: 4-9.
Potential problems: A very fast-spreading plant that will quickly occupy any site or cover a vertical support.
Wildlife value: Fruit, shelter, cover.
Wildlife attracted: Birds, small mammals.

ATTRACTS BUTTERFLIES/MOTHS

ATTRACTS HUMMINGBIRDS

ATTRACTS BIRDS

ATTRACTS SMALL MAMMALS

ATTRACTS LARGE MAMMALS

ATTRACTS BUTTERFLIES/ MOTHS

ATTRACTS HUMMING- BIRDS

ATTRACTS BIRDS

ATTRACTS SMALL MAMMALS

ATTRACTS LARGE MAMMALS

BIG BLUESTEM

Andropogon gerardii
Also known as BEARDGRASS *or*
TURKEY FOOT

Plant type: Native perennial grass.
Bloom season: Late summer into fall.
Flower color: Varies from bronze to purple.
Fruit/seeds: Seeds in fall.
Size: Grows to 6 feet.
Growing preferences: Well-drained, dry soil of low to average fertility in full sun.
Zones: 4-10.
Potential problems: Generally trouble-free.
Wildlife value: Seed, shelter, cover.
Wildlife attracted: Butterflies, moths, hummingbirds.

CYPERUS SEDGE

Carex pseudocyperus

Plant type: Native perennial grasslike plant.
Bloom season: Spring.
Flower color: Yellowish, maturing to brown.
Fruit/seeds: Seeds in summer into fall.
Size: Grows to 3 feet.
Growing preferences: Moist to wet soil of average to high fertility in partial shade.
Zones: 5-9.
Potential problems: Generally trouble-free.
Wildlife value: Nectar, seed, shelter, cover.
Wildlife attracted: Butterflies, moths, hummingbirds, birds, small mammals.

INDIAN GRASS

Sorghastrum nutans

Plant type: Native perennial grass.
Bloom season: Late summer.
Flower color: Golden brown.
Fruit/seeds: Seeds in early fall.
Size: Grows 3 to 5 feet.
Growing preferences: Dry, well-drained soil of low to average fertility in full sun.
Zones: 4-9.
Potential problems: Generally trouble-free.
Wildlife value: Seed, shelter, cover.
Wildlife attracted: Butterflies, moths, hummingbirds, birds, small mammals.

LITTLE BLUESTEM

Schizachyrium scoparium
Also known as BROOMSEDGE,
PRAIRIE BEARDGRASS,
BROOMGRASS *or* WIREGRASS

Plant type: Native perennial grass.
Bloom season: Midsummer into midfall.
Flower color: Reddish brown.
Fruit/seeds: Seeds in fall.
Size: Grows to 5 feet.
Growing preferences: Adaptable to a wide range of soil types, but prefers full sun. In dry-soil areas, it will grow in clumps, but in moister areas, it will grow as sod.
Zones: 3-10.
Potential problems: Generally trouble-free.
Wildlife value: Seed, shelter, cover.
Wildlife attracted: Butterflies, moths, hummingbirds.

SIDEOATS GRAMMA

Bouteloua curtipendula
Also known as TALL GRAMA
GRASS *or* MESQUITE GRASS

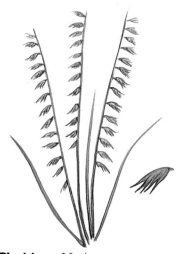

Plant type: Native perennial grass.
Bloom season: Summer.
Flower color: Purple-tinted, maturing to brownish yellow.
Fruit/seeds: Seeds in late summer into fall.
Size: Grows to 2 feet.
Growing preferences: Dry, well-drained soil of average fertility in full sun.
Zones: 4-9.
Potential problems: Generally trouble-free.
Wildlife value: Seed, shelter, cover.
Wildlife attracted: Butterflies, moths, hummingbirds, birds, small mammals, large mammals.

SWITCHGRASS

Panicum virgatum

Plant type: Native perennial grass.
Bloom season: Summer.
Flower color: Purplish, pinkish, reddish or silvery, maturing to brown or grayish white.
Fruit/seeds: Seeds in late summer into fall.
Size: Grows to 7 feet.
Growing preferences: Moist but well-drained soil of average fertility in full sun.
Zones: 5-9.
Potential problems: Generally trouble-free.
Wildlife value: Seed, shelter, cover.
Wildlife attracted: Butterflies, moths, birds, small mammals, large mammals.

ATTRACTS
BUTTERFLIES/
MOTHS

ATTRACTS
HUMMING-
BIRDS

ATTRACTS
BIRDS

ATTRACTS
SMALL
MAMMALS

ATTRACTS
LARGE
MAMMALS

BUNCHBERRY

Cornus canadensis

Plant type: Native deciduous groundcover.

Bloom season: Late spring into early summer.

Flower color: White bracts with green centers.

Fruit/seeds: Red berries in summer into fall.

Size: Grows to 6 inches.

Growing preferences: Moist but well-drained, slightly acid soil in partial shade.

Zones: 2-7.

Potential problems: Generally trouble-free.

Wildlife value: Nectar, fruit, shelter, cover.

Wildlife attracted: Butterflies, moths, hummingbirds, birds, small mammals, large mammals.

CREEPING MAHONIA

Mahonia repens

Plant type: Native evergreen shrub.

Bloom season: Late spring into early summer.

Flower color: Yellow.

Fruit/seeds: Dark blue berries in winter.

Size: Grows to 3 feet.

Growing preferences: Well-drained soil in partial shade, with protection from sun and dry winds during winter.

Zones: 4-7.

Potential problems: Generally trouble-free.

Wildlife value: Nectar, fruit, shelter, cover.

Wildlife attracted: Butterflies, moths, hummingbirds, birds, small mammals.

CREEPING SNOWBERRY

Gaultheria hispidula

Plant type: Native evergreen groundcover.

Bloom season: Late summer.

Flower color: White.

Fruit/seeds: White berries in early fall.

Size: Grows to 6 inches.

Growing preferences: Rich, moist but well-drained soil in shade.

Zones: 4-8.

Potential problems: Generally trouble-free.

Wildlife value: Nectar, fruit, shelter, cover.

Wildlife attracted: Butterflies, moths, hummingbirds, birds, small mammals, large mammals.

PARTRIDGEBERRY

Mitchella repens

Plant type: Native evergreen groundcover.
Bloom season: Early summer.
Flower color: White.
Fruit/seeds: Bright red berries in summer.
Size: Grows to 2 inches.
Growing preferences: Rich, moist but well-drained, acid soil in shade.
Zones: 4-9.
Potential problems: Generally trouble-free.
Wildlife value: Nectar, fruit.
Wildlife attracted: Butterflies, moths, hummingbirds, birds, small mammals, large mammals.

WILD STRAWBERRY

Fragaria virginiana
Also known as VIRGINIA *or* FIELD STRAWBERRY

Plant type: Native deciduous groundcover.
Bloom season: Late spring.
Flower color: White.
Fruit/seeds: Red berries in early summer.
Size: Grows to 6 inches.
Growing preferences: Well-drained soil of average fertility in full sun.
Zones: 5-10.
Potential problems: Generally trouble-free.
Wildlife value: Nectar, fruit.
Wildlife attracted: Butterflies, moths, hummingbirds, birds, small mammals, large mammals.

WINTERGREEN

Gaultheria procumbens
Also known as TEABERRY

Plant type: Native evergreen groundcover.
Bloom season: Late spring to early summer.
Flower color: Pinkish white.
Fruit/seeds: Bright red berries in clusters in late summer into fall.
Size: Grows to 4 inches.
Growing preferences: Moist, acid soil of average fertility in full sun to partial shade.
Zones: 4-8.
Potential problems: Generally trouble-free.
Wildlife value: Nectar, fruit, shelter, cover.
Wildlife attracted: Butterflies, moths, hummingbirds, birds, small mammals.

ATTRACTS BUTTERFLIES/MOTHS

ATTRACTS HUMMINGBIRDS

ATTRACTS BIRDS

ATTRACTS SMALL MAMMALS

ATTRACTS LARGE MAMMALS

ASTILBE

Astilbe × arendsii

Plant type: Perennial.
Bloom season: Late spring to late summer.
Flower color: Red, pink, lilac, peach, maroon or white, depending on the cultivar.
Size: Grows up to 4 feet.
Growing preferences: Rich, moist soil in partial shade.
Zones: 3-9.
Potential problems: Generally trouble-free.
Wildlife value: Nectar.
Wildlife attracted: Butterflies, moths, hummingbirds.

BEE BALM

Monarda didyma
Also known as OSWEGO TEA

Plant type: Native perennial.
Bloom season: Early through late summer.
Flower color: Red, pink, red-violet, purple or white; red cultivars such as 'Adama', 'Cambridge Scarlet' or 'Prairie Glow' attract hummingbirds.
Size: Grows 2 to 4 feet.
Growing preferences: Moist but well-drained soil of rich to average fertility in a sunny to partially shaded location.
Zones: 4-8.
Potential problems: Mildew can strike the plant immediately after it flowers. Control outbreaks by cutting the plant back to the ground and removing all cuttings; new growth will appear quickly.
Wildlife value: Nectar.
Wildlife attracted: Butterflies, moths, hummingbirds.

BEGONIA

Begonia grandis
Also known as HARDY BEGONIA

Plant type: Perennial.
Bloom season: Midsummer through early fall.
Flower color: Pink or white.
Size: Grows to 2 feet.
Growing preferences: Moist but well-drained, slightly sandy soil in partial shade.
Zones: 5-10.
Potential problems: Generally trouble-free.
Wildlife value: Nectar.
Wildlife attracted: Butterflies, moths, hummingbirds.

BLACK-EYED SUSANS

Rudbeckia spp.

Plant type: Native perennials.
Bloom season: Summer through midfall.
Flower color: Yellow with brown center.
Size: Grows 1½ to 6 feet, depending on the species.
Growing preferences: Well-drained, fertile soil in full sun.
Zones: 4-9.
Potential problems: Generally after two or three years of flowering, the plant will lose its vitality and need to be replaced.
Wildlife value: Nectar, seed.
Wildlife attracted: Butterflies, moths, birds, small mammals.

BUTTERFLY WEED

Asclepias tuberosa

Plant type: Native perennial.
Bloom season: Summer.
Flower color: Bright orange, red-orange or yellow-orange.
Size: Grows to 30 inches.
Growing preferences: Well-drained, fertile soil in full sun.
Zones: 3-9.
Potential problems: Generally trouble-free.
Wildlife value: Nectar.
Wildlife attracted: Butterflies, moths, hummingbirds.

CARDINAL FLOWER

Lobelia cardinalis

Plant type: Native perennial.
Bloom season: Mid- to late-summer.
Flower color: Brilliant red.
Size: Grows 2 to 4 feet.
Growing preferences: Moist but well-drained soil in full sun.
Zones: 2-9.
Potential problems: Continuing wet conditions during winter can kill off the plants.
Wildlife value: Nectar.
Wildlife attracted: Butterflies, moths, hummingbirds.

ATTRACTS BUTTERFLIES/ MOTHS

ATTRACTS HUMMING-BIRDS

ATTRACTS BIRDS

ATTRACTS SMALL MAMMALS

ATTRACTS LARGE MAMMALS

ATTRACTS
BUTTERFLIES/
MOTHS

ATTRACTS
HUMMING-
BIRDS

ATTRACTS
BIRDS

ATTRACTS
SMALL
MAMMALS

ATTRACTS
LARGE
MAMMALS

COMMON YARROW

Achillea millefolium

Plant type: Native perennial.
Bloom season: Throughout summer.
Flower color: White.
Size: Grows to 3 feet.
Growing preferences: Moist, rich soil in full sun.
Zones: 3-7.
Potential problems: The species can be invasive; to avoid this problem, plant cultivars instead.
Wildlife value: Nectar.
Wildlife attracted: Butterflies, moths, hummingbirds.

CORAL BELLS

Heuchera sanguinea

Plant type: Native perennial.
Bloom season: Spring, with possible second bloom in summer.
Flower color: Red, pink, peach or white.
Size: Grows to 18 inches.
Growing preferences: Moist but well-drained, rich soil in partial shade.
Zones: 3-8.
Potential problems: Generally trouble-free.
Wildlife value: Nectar.
Wildlife attracted: Butterflies, moths, hummingbirds.

DOGBANES

Apocynum spp.
Also known as INDIAN HEMP

Plant type: Native perennials.
Bloom season: Summer.
Flower color: Pink.
Size: Grows to 4 feet.
Growing preferences: Well-drained soil in full sun.
Zones: 4-9.
Potential problems: Poisonous.
Wildlife value: Nectar.
Wildlife attracted: Butterflies, moths, hummingbirds, birds.

EVENING PRIMROSES/ SUNDROPS

Oenothera spp.

Plant type: Perennials.
Bloom season: Throughout summer (evening primrose blooms at night).
Flower color: Yellow, pink or white.
Fruit/seeds: Seedpods.
Size: Grows to 6 feet.
Growing preferences: Average soil in full sun.
Zones: 3-9.
Potential problems: Can be semi-invasive.
Wildlife value: Nectar, seeds.
Wildlife attracted: Butterflies, moths, hummingbirds, birds, small mammals.

FIREWEED

Epilobium angustifolium

Plant type: Native perennial.
Bloom season: Summer.
Flower color: Pink.
Size: Grows to 5 feet.
Growing preferences: Moist but well-drained soil in full sun.
Zones: 3-7.
Potential problems: Can be invasive, requiring containment.
Wildlife value: Nectar, seed, shelter, cover.
Wildlife attracted: Butterflies, moths, hummingbirds, birds, small mammals.

FOXGLOVE PENSTEMON

Penstemon digitalis
Also known as FOXGLOVE BEARDTONGUE

Plant type: Native perennial.
Bloom season: Late spring.
Flower color: White.
Size: Grows to 5 feet.
Growing preferences: Well-drained, even slightly dry, soil in full sun to partial shade.
Zones: 4-8.
Potential problems: Replace every three or four years to maintain vitality.
Wildlife value: Nectar.
Wildlife attracted: Butterflies, moths, hummingbirds.

ATTRACTS BUTTERFLIES/ MOTHS

ATTRACTS HUMMING-BIRDS

ATTRACTS BIRDS

ATTRACTS SMALL MAMMALS

ATTRACTS LARGE MAMMALS

ATTRACTS
BUTTERFLIES/
MOTHS

ATTRACTS
HUMMING-
BIRDS

ATTRACTS
BIRDS

ATTRACTS
SMALL
MAMMALS

ATTRACTS
LARGE
MAMMALS

GLOBE THISTLE

Echinops ritro

Plant type: Native perennial.
Bloom season: Summer.
Flower color: Pink or purple.
Size: Grows to 4 feet.
Growing preferences: Well-drained, poor soil in full sun.
Zones: 3-8.
Potential problems: Can be invasive, requiring containment.
Wildlife value: Nectar, seed.
Wildlife attracted: Butterflies, moths, hummingbirds, birds, small mammals.

GOLDENRODS

Solidago spp.

Plant type: Native perennials.
Bloom season: Summer into early fall.
Flower color: Yellow.
Size: Grows 1 to 5 feet, depending on the species.
Growing preferences: Well-drained soil in full sun to full shade.
Zones: 3-9.
Potential problems: Generally trouble-free.
Wildlife value: Nectar, seed.
Wildlife attracted: Butterflies, moths, hummingbirds, birds, small mammals, large mammals.

HUMMINGBIRD FLOWER

Zauschneria californica
Also known as CALIFORNIA FUCHSIA

Plant type: Native perennial.
Bloom season: Late summer into early fall.
Flower color: Bright red, borne in clusters.
Size: Grows to 18 inches.
Growing preferences: Well-drained soil in full sun.
Zones: 8-10. Should be considered an annual north of Zone 8.
Potential problems: Generally trouble-free.
Wildlife value: Nectar.
Wildlife attracted: Butterflies, moths, hummingbirds.

INDIAN PAINTBRUSH

Castilleja lanceolata

Plant type: Native perennial.
Bloom season: Summer.
Flower color: Bright red.
Size: Grows to 24 inches.
Growing preferences: Well-drained, rich, slightly sandy soil in full sun to partial shade.
Zones: 5-9.
Potential problems: This is a parasitic plant that is difficult to establish in the backyard habitat. It will weaken other nearby plants by attaching to their roots to establish itself.
Wildlife value: Nectar, seed.
Wildlife attracted: Butterflies, moths, hummingbirds.

IRONWEED

Vernonia noveboracensis

Plant type: Native perennial.
Bloom season: Late summer into midfall.
Flower color: Bright violet.
Size: Grows to 7 feet.
Growing preferences: Moist to wet, rich soil in full sun.
Zones: 5-10.
Potential problems: Generally trouble-free.
Wildlife value: Nectar, seed.
Wildlife attracted: Butterflies, moths, hummingbirds, birds.

LANCE-LEAVED COREOPSIS

Coreopsis lanceolata

Plant type: Native perennial.
Bloom season: Summer.
Flower color: Yellow.
Size: Grows to 2 feet.
Growing preferences: Well-drained, fertile soil in full sun.
Zones: 3-8.
Potential problems: Generally trouble-free.
Wildlife value: Nectar, seed.
Wildlife attracted: Butterflies, moths, hummingbirds, birds, small mammals.

ATTRACTS
BUTTERFLIES/
MOTHS

ATTRACTS
HUMMING-
BIRDS

ATTRACTS
BIRDS

ATTRACTS
SMALL
MAMMALS

ATTRACTS
LARGE
MAMMALS

LEOPARD LILY

Belamcanda chinensis

Plant type: Non-native perennial.
Bloom season: Throughout summer.
Flower color: Orange with brownish spots.
Fruit/seeds: Large seedpods with shiny black seeds.
Size: Grows to 3 feet.
Growing preferences: Rich, well-drained soil in full sun.
Zones: 4-10.
Potential problems: May be attacked by iris borers and foliar leafspot.
Wildlife value: Nectar, seeds.
Wildlife attracted: Butterflies, moths, hummingbirds, birds, small mammals.

LOBELIAS

Lobelia spp.
See also CARDINAL FLOWER *on page* 143

Plant type: Perennials.
Bloom season: Mid- to late-summer.
Flower color: Bright red, blue or purple.
Size: Grows to 3 feet.
Growing preferences: Moist but well-drained, rich soil in full sun.
Zones: 4-9.
Potential problems: Generally trouble-free.
Wildlife value: Nectar.
Wildlife attracted: Butterflies, moths, hummingbirds

LUPINES

Lupinus spp.

Plant type: Native perennials.
Bloom season: Late spring through summer.
Flower color: Orange, red, pink, purple or white, depending on the cultivar.
Size: Grows to 4 feet.
Growing preferences: Well-drained, alkaline soil in full sun to partial shade.
Zones: 5-9.
Potential problems: Can be invasive, spreading freely through self-sown seedlings.
Wildlife value: Nectar, seed.
Wildlife attracted: Butterflies, moths, hummingbirds.

MILKWEEDS

Asclepias spp.
See also BUTTERFLY WEED *on* page 143.

Plant type: Native perennials.
Bloom season: Summer.
Flower color: Pink to rose-purple.
Size: Grows 1 to 5 feet.
Growing preferences: Well-drained, fertile soil in full sun.
Zones: 3-9.
Potential problems: Can be invasive, requiring containment.
Wildlife value: Nectar, seed.
Wildlife attracted: Butterflies, moths.

MINTS

Mentha spp.

Plant type: Native perennials.
Bloom season: Summer.
Flower color: Pink or purple.
Size: Grows to 24 inches.
Growing preferences: Well-drained, average to poor soil in full sun.
Zones: 4-9.
Potential problems: Can be invasive, requiring containment.
Wildlife value: Nectar.
Wildlife attracted: Butterflies, moths, hummingbirds.

NEW ENGLAND ASTER

Aster novae-angliae

Plant type: Native perennial.
Bloom season: Fall.
Flower color: Pink, cherry-red, purple or white.
Size: Grows to 30 inches.
Growing preferences: Moist but well-drained soil in full to partial shade.
Zones: 3-8.
Potential problems: Mildew.
Wildlife value: Nectar, seed, shelter, cover.
Wildlife attracted: Butterflies, moths, hummingbirds, birds, small mammals.

ATTRACTS BUTTERFLIES/ MOTHS

ATTRACTS HUMMING-BIRDS

ATTRACTS BIRDS

ATTRACTS SMALL MAMMALS

ATTRACTS LARGE MAMMALS

ATTRACTS BUTTERFLIES/ MOTHS

ATTRACTS HUMMING- BIRDS

ATTRACTS BIRDS

ATTRACTS SMALL MAMMALS

ATTRACTS LARGE MAMMALS

ORANGE CONEFLOWER

Rudbeckia fulgida
See also BLACK-EYED SUSANS *on page 143*

Plant type: Native perennial.
Bloom season: Late summer to early fall.
Flower color: Yellow-orange with black centers.
Size: Grows to 3 feet.
Growing preferences: Moist soil in full sun to partial shade.
Zones: 3-9.
Potential problems: Generally trouble-free.
Wildlife value: Nectar, seed.
Wildlife attracted: Butterflies, moths, hummingbirds.

PURPLE CONEFLOWER

Echinacea purpurea

Plant type: Native perennial.
Bloom season: Summer.
Flower color: Mauve with orange-brown center.
Size: Grows to 4 feet.
Growing preferences: Moist but well-drained, rich soil in full sun.
Zones: 4-8.
Potential problems: Generally trouble-free.
Wildlife value: Nectar, seed.
Wildlife attracted: Butterflies, moths, hummingbirds, birds.

RED CLOVER

Trifolium pratense

Plant type: Perennial.
Bloom season: Summer.
Flower color: Various shades of rose-purple.
Size: Grows to 2 feet.
Growing preferences: Moist but well-drained soil of average to high fertility in full sun.
Zones: 4-9.
Potential problems: Sometimes difficult to get seed to set due to insect problems.
Wildlife value: Nectar.
Wildlife attracted: Butterflies, moths, hummingbirds, birds, small mammals, large mammals.

RED-HOT POKER

Kniphofia uvaria
Also known as TORCH LILY

Plant type: Native perennial.
Bloom season: Late spring into summer.
Flower color: Bright red, turning yellow with age.
Size: Grows to 5 feet.
Growing preferences: Constantly moist soil of average fertility in full sun.
Zones: 5-9.
Potential problems: Generally trouble-free.
Wildlife value: Nectar, seed.
Wildlife attracted: Butterflies, moths, hummingbirds, birds, small mammals.

SCARLET MONKEY FLOWER

Mimulus cardinalis

Plant type: Native perennial.
Bloom season: Summer.
Flower color: Red.
Size: Grows to 12 inches.
Growing preferences: Moist to wet, rich soil in full sun.
Zones: 9-11. Can be grown as an annual north of Zone 9.
Potential problems: Generally trouble-free.
Wildlife value: Nectar, seed.
Wildlife attracted: Butterflies, moths, hummingbirds, birds, small mammals.

SCARLET SAGE

Salvia splendens

Plant type: Native perennial.
Bloom season: Summer into early fall.
Flower color: Bright red.
Size: Grows to 12 inches.
Growing preferences: Rich, well-drained soil in full sun.
Zones: 10-11. Can be grown as an annual north of zone 10.
Potential problems: Can be slow-growing.
Wildlife value: Nectar.
Wildlife attracted: Butterflies, moths, hummingbirds, birds, small mammals.

ATTRACTS BUTTERFLIES/ MOTHS

ATTRACTS HUMMING-BIRDS

ATTRACTS BIRDS

ATTRACTS SMALL MAMMALS

ATTRACTS LARGE MAMMALS

SHOWY SEDUM

Sedum spectabile
Also known as ICE PLANT *and*
SHOWY STONECROP

Plant type: Native, semi-evergreen perennial.
Bloom season: Late summer.
Flower color: Pink or red.
Size: Grows to 2 feet.
Growing preferences: Well-drained soil of average to high fertility in full sun.
Zones: 3-9.
Potential problems: Generally trouble-free.
Wildlife value: Nectar, seed.
Wildlife attracted: Butterflies, moths, hummingbirds, birds, small mammals.

SNEEZEWEED

Helenium autumnale
Also known as HELEN'S FLOWER

Plant type: Native perennial.
Bloom season: Late summer to fall.
Flower color: Yellow or orange.
Size: Grows to 5 feet.
Growing preferences: Well-drained soil of average fertility in full sun.
Zones: 3-8.
Potential problems: Generally trouble-free.
Wildlife value: Nectar, shelter, cover.
Wildlife attracted: Butterflies, moths, hummingbirds, birds, small mammals.

WILD BERGAMOT

Monarda fistulosa

Plant type: Native perennial.
Bloom season: Mid- to late-summer.
Flower color: Pink or lavender.
Size: Grows to 4 feet.
Growing preferences: Moist but well-drained soil of average fertility in full sun.
Zones: 3-9.
Potential problems: May be attracted by powdery mildew.
Wildlife value: Nectar, seed.
Wildlife attracted: Butterflies, moths, hummingbirds, birds, small mammals.

WILD BLUE PHLOX

Phlox divaricata

Plant type: Native perennial.
Bloom season: Early summer.
Flower color: Purplish blue, pale blue or white.
Size: Grows to 15 inches.
Growing preferences: Rich, moist but well-drained soil in partial shade.
Zones: 3-9.
Potential problems: Generally trouble-free.
Wildlife value: Nectar, seed.
Wildlife attracted: Butterflies, moths, hummingbirds, birds, small mammals.

WILD COLUMBINE

Aquilegia canadensis
Also known as COMMON
COLUMBINE

Plant type: Native perennial.
Bloom season: Spring and early summer.
Flower color: Red and yellow.
Size: Grows 1 to 3 feet.
Growing preferences: Well-drained soil of average fertility in full sun.
Zones: 3-8.
Potential problems: Leafminers, aphids.
Wildlife value: Nectar, seed.
Wildlife attracted: Butterflies, moths, hummingbirds, birds, small mammals.

YELLOW TROUT LILY

Erythronium americanum
Also known as FAWN LILY

Plant type: Native perennial.
Bloom season: Spring.
Flower color: Yellow to bronze.
Size: Grows to 10 inches.
Growing preferences: Moist but well-drained, rich soil in partial shade.
Zones: 3-8.
Potential problems: Bulbs must be kept from drying out during the summer.
Wildlife value: Nectar.
Wildlife attracted: Butterflies, moths, hummingbirds.

ATTRACTS
BUTTERFLIES/
MOTHS

ATTRACTS
HUMMING-
BIRDS

ATTRACTS
BIRDS

ATTRACTS
SMALL
MAMMALS

ATTRACTS
LARGE
MAMMALS

ATTRACTS
BUTTERFLIES/
MOTHS

ATTRACTS
HUMMING-
BIRDS

ATTRACTS
BIRDS

ATTRACTS
SMALL
MAMMALS

ATTRACTS
LARGE
MAMMALS

AGERATUM

Ageratum houstonianum
Also known as FLOSSFLOWER

Plant type: Annual.
Bloom season: Summer.
Flower color: Pink, blue or white, depending on the cultivar.
Size: Grows to 14 inches.
Growing preferences: Rich, moist but well-drained soil in full sun.
Potential problems: The number of flowers will be reduced if the plant is allowed to dry out after growth begins.
Wildlife value: Nectar, seed.
Wildlife attracted: Butterflies, moths, hummingbirds.

COMMON SUNFLOWER

Helianthus annuus
Also known as SUNFLOWER

Plant type: Annual.
Bloom season: Late summer.
Flower color: Yellow petals around extremely large center that is black when mature.
Fruit/seeds: Black or striped seeds in great profusion.
Size: Grows to 12 feet.
Growing preferences: Well-drained soil of average fertility in full sun.
Potential problems: Can become invasive in the second year if seeds are allowed to fall to the ground.
Wildlife value: Nectar, seed.
Wildlife attracted: Butterflies, moths, hummingbirds, birds, small mammals, large mammals.

COSMOS

Cosmos spp.

Plant type: Annuals.
Bloom season: Summer into early fall.
Flower color: Red, orange or yellow, or pink, maroon or white, depending on the species and cultivar.
Size: Grows to 6 feet.
Growing preferences: Moist but well-drained soil of average to high fertility in full sun.
Potential problems: Generally trouble-free.
Wildlife value: Nectar, seed.
Wildlife attracted: Butterflies, moths, hummingbirds, birds, small mammals.

FLOWERING TOBACCO

Nicotiana alata
Also known as NICOTIANA

Plant type: Annual.
Bloom season: Late summer.
Flower color: Creamy white, green, red, maroon or pink.
Size: Grows to 30 inches.
Growing preferences: Well-drained, fertile soil in full sun.
Potential problems: Generally trouble-free.
Wildlife value: Nectar.
Wildlife attracted: Butterflies, moths, hummingbirds.

HELIOTROPE

Heliotropium arborescens
Also known as COMMON
HELIOTROPE *or* CHERRY-PIE

Plant type: Annual.
Bloom season: Summer.
Flower color: Purple or white.
Size: Grows to 4 feet.
Growing preferences: Rich, well-drained soil in full sun.
Potential problems: In hot-summer areas, prefers afternoon shade.
Wildlife value: Nectar.
Wildlife attracted: Butterflies, moths, hummingbirds.

QUEEN-ANNE'S-LACE

Daucus carota var. *carota*

Plant type: Biennial.
Bloom season: Summer.
Flower color: White.
Size: Grows to 3 feet.
Growing preferences: Well-drained soil of average fertility in full sun.
Zones: 5-10.
Potential problems: Can be extremely invasive, requiring containment.
Wildlife value: Nectar, seed.
Wildlife attracted: Butterflies, moths, hummingbirds.

ATTRACTS
BUTTERFLIES/
MOTHS

ATTRACTS
HUMMING-
BIRDS

ATTRACTS
BIRDS

ATTRACTS
SMALL
MAMMALS

ATTRACTS
LARGE
MAMMALS

TICKSEED SUNFLOWER

Bidens aristosa

Plant type: Native annual.
Bloom season: Late summer into fall.
Flower color: Yellow.
Size: Grows to 3 feet.
Growing preferences: Moist soil of average fertility in full sun to partial shade.
Potential problems: The plant does not do well in competition with other species.
Wildlife value: Nectar, seed.
Wildlife attracted: Butterflies, moths, hummingbirds, birds, small mammals.

VERBENA

Verbena × hybrida
Also known as GARDEN VERBENA

Plant type: Annual.
Bloom season: Summer into early fall.
Flower color: Pink, white, red, purple or yellow.
Size: Grows to 12 inches.
Growing preferences: Well-drained soil of average fertility in full sun.
Potential problems: Generally trouble-free.
Wildlife value: Nectar, seed.
Wildlife attracted: Butterflies, moths, hummingbirds, birds, small mammals.

ZINNIA

Zinnia elegans

Plant type: Annual.
Bloom season: Summer into early fall.
Flower color: Purple, red, orange, yellow, pink, white, green or striped.
Size: Grows to 3 feet.
Growing preferences: Rich, moist but well-drained soil in full sun.
Potential problems: Regular deadheading is essential to keep plants blooming all season. Powdery mildew may attack foliage.
Wildlife value: Nectar, seed.
Wildlife attracted: Butterflies, moths, hummingbirds.

RECOMMENDED READING

Adams, George. *Birdscaping Your Garden.* Emmaus, Pa.: Rodale Press, 1994.

Art, Henry, W. *A Garden of Wildflowers.* Storey Communications Inc.: Pownal, Vt. 1986.

The Audubon Society Field Guide series. Alfred A. Knopf, New York.

Brown, Tom, Jr. *Tom Brown's Field Guide to the Forgotten Wilderness.* Berkley Publishing Group: New York, 1987.

Cox, Jeff. *Landscaping with Nature.* Emmaus, Pa.: Rodale Press, 1991.

Curtis, Will and Jane. *Backyard Bird Habitat.* Countryman Press Inc.: Woodstock, Vt., 1988.

Daniels, Stevie. *The Wild Lawn Handbook.* Macmillan Publishing Co.: New York, 1995.

Druse, Ken, and Margaret Roach. *The Natural Habitat Garden.* Crown Publishing Group: New York, 1994.

Harrison, Hal. *A Field Guide to Birds' Nests.* Houghton Mifflin Co.: Boston, 1988.

Heriteau, Jacqueline, and Charles B. Thomas. *Water Gardens.* Houghton Mifflin Co.: Boston, 1994.

Martin, Alexander C., Herbert S. Zim, and Arnold L. Nelson. *American Wildlife & Plants: A Guide to Wildlife Food Habits.* Dover Publications, Inc.: New York, 1951.

Martin, Laura C. *The Wildflower Meadow Book,* 2nd ed. Globe Pequot Press, Old Saybrook, Ct.: 1986.

McCord, Nancy. *Please Don't Eat My Garden.* Sterling Publishing Co., Inc.: New York, 1992.

Michalak, Patricia S., and Linda A. Gilkeson. *Rodale's Successful Organic Gardening: Controlling Pests and Diseases.* Rodale Press: Emmaus, Pa., 1994.

Organic Gardening magazine, Rodale Press, Inc., 33 E. Minor St., Emmaus, Pa. 18098.

The Peterson Field Guide series, Houghton Mifflin Co., Boston.

Phillips, Roger, and Martyn Rix. *The Random House Book of Shrubs.* Random House: New York, 1989.

Schneck, Marcus. *The Bird Feeder Guide.* Dorset Press: New York, 1989.

–. *Butterflies: How to Identify and Attract Them to Your Garden.* Emmaus, Pa.: Rodale Press, 1990.

–. *Your Backyard Wildlife Garden.* Rodale Press: Emmaus, Pa., 1992.

Sternberg, Guy, and Jim Wilson. *Landscaping with Native Trees.* Chapters Publishing Ltd.: Shelburne, Vt., 1995.

The Stokes Nature Guide Series, Little, Brown and Co., Boston.

Thomas, Charles B. *Creating Your Own Water Garden.* Storey Communications Inc.: Pownal, Vt. 1991.

Tuttle, Merlin D. *America's Neighborhood Bats.* University of Texas Press: Austin, Tex., 1988.

U.S. Department of Agriculture staff. *Common Weeds of the United States.* Dover Publications, Inc.: New York, 1970.

Wieser, K. H., and Dr. P. V. Loiselle. *Your Garden Pond.* Tetra Press: Blacksburg, Va., 1989.

RESOURCES FOR WILDLIFE HABITATS

American Birding Association
P.O. Box 6599
Colorado Springs, CO 80934

Backyard Wildlife Network
1328 Chestnut Street #393
Emmaus, PA 18049

Bat Conservation International
P.O. Box 162603
Austin, TX 78716

Hawk Mountain Sanctuary Association
Route 2, Box 191
Kempton, PA 19529

Laboratory of Ornithology
Cornell University
159 Sapsucker Woods Road
Ithaca, NY 14850

National Audubon Society
700 Broadway
New York, NY 10003

National Wildlife Federation
Backyard Wildlife Habitat Program
1400 16th Street NW
Washington, DC 20036

National Wildflower Research Organization
2600 FM 973 North
Austin, TX 78725

North American Bluebird Society
P.O. Box 6295
Silver Spring, MD 20916-6295

U.S. Fish & Wildlife Service
1849 C Street NW
Washington, DC 20240

Wildlife Habitat Canada
7 Hinton Avenue N, Suite 200
Ottawa, Ontario
Canada K1Y 4P1

Wildlife Habitat Council
1010 Wayne Avenue, Suite 920
Silver Spring, MD 20910

INDEX

ACKNOWLEDGMENTS

Quarto Publishing would like to thank the following for supplying pictures for this book:
Key: *a* = above, *b* = below, *l* = left, *r* = right, *c* = center

Richard Day/Daybreak Imagery 15*b*, 51*a* & *b*, 73, 87*b*, 96, 103, 113*l*, *c*, & *r*, 121*l*; **Photo/Nats** (Liz Ball) 74, 94, (Jean T. Buermeyer) 67*r*, (Gay Bumgarner) 12, 80*a*, 89*r*, 95, (Priscilla Connell) 37, 63*r*, 78, (Tim Daniel) 53, 101, 109, (Carl Hanninen) 16, (Edward Hodgson) 63*l*, (Don Johnston) 45*l*, 91, (Sydney Karp) 44, (Stephen G. Maka) 66, 83, 86*r*, (David M. Stone) 49, (Muriel V. Williams) 99; **Leonard Lee Rue** 15*a*, 20, 33, 38*l*, 41, 51*c*, 77, (Irene

Vanermolen) 79, 85*r*, 87*a*, 89*l*, 92, 110, 111, 118; **Marcus Schneck** 38*c* & *r*, 47, 57, 64, 65, 67*l*, 84; **Gregory K. Scott** 17, 27*l* & *r*, 28, 31, 45*r*, 48, 61, 68, 71, 80*b*, 86*l*, 117, 121*r*; **Scott Weidensaul** 23; **Bill Beatty/Wild & Natural** 85*l*.

While every effort has been made to trace and acknowledge all copyright holders we would like to apologize should any omissions have been made.

All other images are the copyright of Quarto Publishing.

Index by Susan Hibbert